# INTERVENTION SKILLS

# INTERVENTION SKILLS

## Process Consultation *for* Small Groups and Teams

### W. BRENDAN REDDY, Ph.D.

*Foreword by J. William Pfeiffer, Ph.D., J.D.*

JOSSEY-BASS/PFEIFFER
A Wiley Company
www.pfeiffer.com

Published by

## JOSSEY-BASS/PFEIFFER
A Wiley Company
989 Market Street
San Francisco, CA 94103-1741
415.433.1740; Fax 415.433.0499
800.274.4434; Fax 800.569.0443

www.pfeiffer.com

Jossey-Bass/Pfeiffer is a registered trademark of John Wiley & Sons, Inc.

ISBN: 0-88390-434-9
Library of Congress Catalog Card Number 94-065468

Printed in the United States of America

Printing  10  9  8  7  6  5  4  3

We at Jossey-Bass strive to use the most environmentally sensitive paper stocks available to us. Our publications are printed on acid-free recycled stock whenever possible, and our paper always meets or exceeds minimum GPO and EPA requirements.

# Dedication

*I call to the distant running boy.*
*He does not hear.*

*I turn from catching toads*
*To see you watching me.*

*Smiling, you reach out*
*And bring me home.*

From: "Reflections"
(Reddy, 1969)

# Acknowledgments

*F*ew books are written without the help, assistance, and contributions of many people. First, I want to thank my graduate students at the University of Cincinnati and the many participants of public and in-house group process consultation seminars and workshops. Their experiences, ideas, and feedback form the fabric of this book.

Editor Mary Kitzmiller was most affirming and then added the right words in the right places in the manuscript.

My wife, Vivian, and daughter, Ceallaigh, were infinitely patient with my ranting and raving about this book—and the time involved. Ready for the next one?

A very special thanks goes to my friend, colleague, and business partner, Chuck Phillips, consultant *extraordinaire,* for his support and contribution to the development of this book. We spent many hours in discussion and in workshops, practicing and challenging the concepts, ideas, and skills contained in this book.

Finally, to Leonard D. Goodstein—friend, colleague, and mentor—whose wisdom, help, and admonitions have been there for me, personally and professionally, throughout my career—a rare gift indeed: Thank you.

# Foreword

*The* book you are about to read—and study and use as a reference for years to come—was written by a true expert in consulting skills. Whether you are launching a career as a process consultant or desiring to increase the skills you have used over the years or attempting to teach others how to improve their skills, you will find this book invaluable.

*Intervention Skills* deals with interventions in small groups and teams, defined as up to twelve members. As Dr. Reddy states in the Introduction, many practitioners understand the theory but are hard pressed to know exactly what to say and do, or not to say and do, in situations that require interventions. After many successful years of working with small groups, the author has been able to determine the situations the consultant will encounter most frequently. His book explains exactly how to intervene in these situations and gives specific examples of the most appropriate responses.

This is a practical book: easy-to-read, concrete, and immediately useful to the reader. Although the author gives ample theoretical background and context, the novice will not be intimidated, and the experienced practitioner will be spurred on to even greater success.

*Intervention Skills* is a must for every person whose career involves working with groups. I predict that this book will become the classic resource in process consultation.

—J. William Pfeiffer, Ph.D., J.D.
President, Pfeiffer & Company
February, 1994

# Contents

# Introduction

*The* desire to write a book about the micro world of group process consultation emerged from years of consulting to both for-profit and not-for-profit organizations; conducting in-house training and public seminars for both managers and consultants; and training graduate students in organization development and consultation. In each instance, participants understood broad-based theory, yet responded with, "...but how do I *really* intervene here?" or "What should I *actually* say or do?" Indeed, they had reason to wonder. Although the practitioner or manager could sometimes produce a desired end behavior, he or she was hard pressed to show micro steps and specific behaviors or interventions required to reach that desired end.

The gap between theory-in-use and espoused theory (Argyris, 1970) was often one of lack of skill training. In addition, it was obvious that some managers, consultants, or trainers were "on target" much of the time or their "presentation of self" (Goffman, 1973) compensated for premature, misinterventions, and lack of theoretical framework. While the "flying-by-the-seat-of-the-pants" school of training, managing, and consulting has many students in this country, I am instead speaking of the practitioner who seems to be able to "intuit" the most effective intervention.

Conversely, there are those managers, consultants, and trainers who are steeped in theory and technology but whose interventions are minimally impactful. Thus, what evolved was a micro approach to process consultation, that is, (1) an integrated framework around which to make specific interventions; (2) the nature and depth of the interventions; and (3) the character, style, and role of the person who is the practitioner.

## WHO SHOULD READ THIS BOOK

This book is written for anyone who has a role and responsibilities in small groups. The small group is defined here as numbering from four to about twelve members with a common objective. Beyond a dozen or so members, the group dynamics become more complex and are quite different from those in the small group. Small groups include teams, staffs, task groups, quality circles, boards, ad hoc groups, etc. The membership of the small group may include manager, leader, followers, and consultant.

When I began working in the area of group process consultation, I focused on the role of the consultant. It soon became clear, however, for the reasons I have touched on, the manager *and the group members*—as well as the consultant—make interventions into the ongoing life or process of the group. It behooves each of them to be role effective. Still, this book primarily targets the person *in contracted role* as group process consultant. It is he or she who has major responsibility for the *functioning* of the group, at least temporarily.

The term *process consultation* is bandied about by group leaders, members, and consultants. Curiously, little has actually been written on the subject. Edgar Schein's (1987; 1988) two excellent volumes are best known; Goodstein (1978) devotes a chapter to process consultation; and Blake and Mouton (1983) and Huse (1980) also discuss the area. In all of these references, however, process consultation is broadly defined. For example, Schein (1969, p. 9) defines process consultation as "a set of activities on the part of the consultant which helps the client to perceive, understand, and act upon process events which occur in the client's environment."

Process consultation is often confused with the general concept of organization development. In the present book, a more bounded, or *micro* view of process consultation is presented. That is, a group perspective that takes into account small and specific steps, behaviors, and strategies that can serve to direct the "process person" to his or her next step and that effectively moves the group toward task accomplishment and member satisfaction.

## ARRANGEMENT OF BOOK

The book is arranged in nine chapters that parallel the flow of group process consultation. Three comparative cases are followed throughout the book. Intervention-considerations insets offer guides to the reader.

## Chapter One

In Chapter One, group process consultation is explained through definition and the reasons for using a consultant. The phases in the consultation practice are traced in overview and the question of who does group process consultation explored. Group process consultation rests on a solid philosophical base. It is helpful to the group process consultant to have a sense of that foundation.

## Chapter Two

A key set of concepts—process, task, and maintenance—is critical to understanding and serving as a group process consultant. Task is the "how" that refers to getting the job done. Maintenance is the "how" that is concerned with satisfying group members' socioemotional needs. Chapter Two introduces or reacquaints the reader with this critical concept.

## Chapter Three

The first major phase of group consultation, *entry*, is examined in Chapter Three. Three subphases (contract, assessment, and education) are detailed.

## Chapter Four

Chapter Four presents Phase Two, *work proper,* through its subphases: climate setting, vision/mission, and work proper.

## Chapter Five

Group process consultants know there are various types of interventions, but often do not have a systematic way of accessing those interventions. Least known is at what depth to make an intervention. Chapter Five examines both the type and depth of intervention. This chapter serves as the book's fulcrum and contains concepts critical to the understanding of group process consultation.

**Chapter Six**

Although there are several theories of group development, most were developed from university courses in group dynamics. Chapter Six presents a model of work-group activity from the vantage point of the group process consultant. The model helps the consultant know what task/maintenance dynamics are in the foreground and on which of these he or she should intervene.

**Chapter Seven**

What are the competencies required of the group process consultant? Often consultants fall into or are placed in the role without thought of basic competencies. Chapter Seven articulates those elements.

**Chapter Eight**

Does group process consultation have a credible and visible role in the organization? And does it have a future? These questions along with value and ethical considerations are discussed in Chapter Eight.

**Chapter Nine**

Chapter Nine is a potpourri of issues and concerns central to the group process consultant. Questions frequently asked by group process consultants are answered in this chapter; for example, "What are common consultant errors? How do you deal with difficult participants?" Lastly, some rules of thumb are offered.

# What Is Group Process Consultation?

# 1

*In* attempting to understand group process consultation, consider the following three situations.

## *Executive Planning Team* ♦ ♦ ♦

A senior manager is charged with developing a new product line with the intent of regaining market share. The importance to organizational profitability is obvious. He has a group of nine cross-functional managers at his disposal. All are white male. They anticipate convening once a week for two hours over the next six months in planning sessions. These are talented people with big egos. Turfs are fiercely protected. The group members will be spending much time together; tensions will be high. Although working on the tasks will be important, members' task skills vary considerably. Both individual and group needs will have to be dealt with. Finally, the level of interpersonal skills are less than one might expect from such a high-powered group. The senior manager needs help and consultation with this challenge, but where can he go and whom does he ask?

## Quality Circles ♦ ♦ ♦

The vice president of a small Midwest manufacturing organization learned about quality circles in the airline magazine as she flew from Houston to Cincinnati. Upon returning, the VP directed the human resources manager to initiate three groups in the company, reminding the manager that limited funds were available for training. Three quality circle "leaders" were sent off site for a day of training. Hearing of the circles, some employees volunteered for membership; others were pressured to join. Within a month, the three teams were bogged down and unproductive. The leaders had led them through task steps, such as agenda and problem identification, but clearly, there was a range of unexpressed feelings and conflicts. Two of the leaders became aware that covert issues might be interfering with task accomplishment. The third continued to micromanage the group. The leaders were baffled as to what to do next. They feared emotions might erupt and felt they were not equipped to handle them. Moreover, they feared their own emotional expression and questioned its appropriateness.

## Hospital Administration ♦ ♦ ♦

Impacted by competition, recession, and eroding services, the executive group of a rural hospital administration decided to dramatically change the culture of the organization and the way in which business was conducted. The only agreement they had, however, was that change must take place for the hospital to survive. Seth (the chief executive officer), Ned, Jeremy, Ted, Theresa, and Lucia have histories together, coalitions, enmities, and differing views about direction. They understand if this group cannot get its act together, needed change will not take place within the hospital. They have been working for over a month but have not been productive. As a group they lack skill in both managing tasks and managing conflict, upon which they spend a great deal of time. Now they are saying, "We thought we could sit down, put our conflicts aside, and solve the problems so we could move on. We had no idea it would be so difficult."

## Commonalities ◆ ◆ ◆

What do these three scenarios have in common? In each there is a group whose charge is important to the organization either through innovation, profitability, change, or all three. The groups are composed of different people with very different ideas and views, but each person's contribution and input is important. In all likelihood, the groups will exist for a fairly long time. In each there is a necessity for high interaction and creative problem solving and thus the potential for interpersonal tensions and the dynamics of confrontation. Finally, each could use the help of a group process consultant, one who works with the group over an extended period of time. We will return to these groups as we unfold the variables, conditions, and distinctions of group process consultation.

In this chapter we will explore what is group process consultation, its philosophical underpinnings, what differentiates the role from that of other change agents. Finally, the flow of group process consultation is offered as a quasi-structured way of proceeding.

## DEFINING GROUP PROCESS CONSULTATION

Picture any of the scenarios above or a group or team to which you belong as member or manager. The group problem or task is such that high levels of interaction and contribution are required of members to reach a solution. The group process consultant sits in with the group as a member, with a special role, and intervenes while the group is working. An *intervention* refers to *any* comment, suggestion, or recommendation that the consultant makes to the group in the service of accomplishing the task. Group process consultation is a *micro* approach to working in groups. It is the detailed exploration, analysis, and assessment of what is happening as the group members work in the moment. It is the formulation of immediate interventions, putting them into action, while considering what form they should take and with what desired impact.

I contrast this *micro* approach to Edgar Schein's *macro* approach to process consultation. In Schein's revised edition of his seminal work, he defines process consultation as "a set of activities on the part of the consultant that help the client perceive, understand, and act upon the process events that occur in the client's environment in order to improve the situation as defined by the client" (Schein, 1988, p. 11).

Schein describes the *historical* roots of process consultation as anchored in group dynamics and small group processes, but his definition does not mention small group processes. After reviewing observations he has made over the last thirty years about the process of helping human systems, Schein (1990, p. 57) is more explicit and disavows the small-group focus: "I say human *systems* rather than individuals or small groups because much of my work as a consultant has been with intergroup and organizational-level problems."

Schein continues with, "I make this point at the outset because process consultation has been stereotyped as something one does with apparently small groups." Yet, there is a need for a variant of process consultation in which one deals exclusively with small groups. Macro process consultation has evolved to connote intervening in *any* part of the organization. It is often used synonymously for organization development.

The present book is a *micro* approach to process consultation. The focus, explicitly, is the small group. The definition I propose returns us to the small-group environment and the work of the process consultant in the life of that group:

> **Group process consultation** is the reasoned and intentional interventions by the consultant, into the *ongoing* events and dynamics of a group with the purpose of helping that group effectively attain its agreed-upon objectives.

"Reasoned and intentional" means that the consultant's interventions are thought out and directed at a particular target (group, interpersonal, personal) with a specific purpose and desired intensity of impact.

The consultant intervenes into the *ongoing* events and dynamics of the group, whenever he or she feels that it is appropriate to do so. He or she does not wait until the meeting ends and then present data or an alternative. Effective feedback to the group members is *immediate* and timely. Generally, to wait is to lose the moment—and the impact.

The consultant intervenes within the context of the group's *agreed-upon objectives,* that is, the vision, mission, and/or goals on which the group has agreed. The consultant must first help the group articulate what is its primary objective. Without a clear and agreed-upon mission, the consultant will not have a context within which to make his or her interventions.

---

### Intervention Consideration

*Large Group Dynamics.* We sometimes think a group is a group is a group...but the size of the group alone changes the dynamics. Small groups cease being small at about twelve members. Consensus decision making is difficult enough within that number; but beyond that, true consensus is all but impossible. There is greater fragmentation in large groups, a loss of identity by members, and what Bibb Latane called *social loafing* (Latane, Williams, & Harkins, 1979). That is, even competent group members let someone else do the work. Group process consultation does not work well in large groups. If you must work with a large group, break it into small work groups that report back to the larger body. The group is manageable that way.

---

## PHILOSOPHICAL UNDERPINNINGS

The philosophical tenets of group process consultation are consistent with a helping and collaboration model. The consultant is available and focused to help the group become as effective and efficient in reaching whatever vision it has created, the mission it has defined, or the goals it has set. What is an *effective* group? Hackman (1983) defines effectiveness as involving organizational standards, member satisfaction, and the predilection of members to work over time. In his three-dimensional conception of group effectiveness Hackman states:

> First is the degree to which the group's productive output (that is, its product, service, or decision) meets the standards of quantity, quality, and timeliness of the people who receive, review, and/or use that output.
>
> The second dimension is the degree to which the process of carrying out the work enhances the capability of members to work together interdependently in the future.
>
> The third dimension is the degree to which the group experiences contribute to the growth and personal well-being of team members. (pp. 6-7)

This concept is critical to competent group process consultation. It points the consultant toward his or her interventions. Results, task, and output are not the only foci of interventions by the consultant. Indeed, group members' dynamic interactions and their personal well-being take on equal importance. This is consistent with Schein's (1990) general philosophy of helping, "a central concern of the consultant should be to improve the ability of clients themselves..." (p. 57).

The aim, over time, is that the process consultant's actions and interventions provide an implicit operational model for group members. The group members imitate and learn the process interventions and experience and internalize the resultant benefits. As members manage their work over the life of the group, there is less need for the consultant to make interventions. In a sense, the consultant works himself or herself out of a job. Heider (1985), in a wonderful book for leaders and facilitators, drawn from the *I-Ching* of Lao Tse, describes the phenomenon. I have substituted "group process consultant" for Heider's "leader."

## The Group Process Consultant

A group process consultant is best
When people barely know s/he exists.

Not so good when people obey and acclaim her/him.
Worse when they despise her/him.
"Fail to honor people,
they fail to honor you";
But of a good group process consultant,
who talks little,
When her/his work is done,
her/his aim fulfilled,
They will say, "We did this ourselves."

It is intended that participants take on more of the processing themselves. At an overt level, group members may become quite adept at making interventions, self-disclosing, and facing issues. However, at covert levels, the information is less accessible to the untrained and typically requires the group process consultant to continue to make interventions, although fewer in number.

Equifinality, a concept drawn from systems theory, states that the same result may be reached by many different paths. The group process consultant helps the group create its own path. If a group or team is to grow, mature, and become effective, it must develop a sense of identity, awareness of its unique composition, skills, autonomy, and idiosyncratic procedures. A highly productive group or team is greater than the sum of its parts. It is the process consultant who assists the group in understanding and using its dynamics.

The group process consultant is in a unique member role, both dynamically and authoritatively. Attributions are made to him or her. The consultant's decisions about interventions are rooted in his or her history and style. Thus, self-knowledge is important for the group process consultant. If a consultant experiences difficulty in surfacing and managing conflict, for example, he or she may render the group ineffective by colluding in ignoring tensions or even keeping agendas hidden. Likewise, the group process consultant may tend to smooth over group issues that he or she may personally find difficult to handle.

## THE FLOW OF PROCESS CONSULTATION

An overview of the flow of process consultation is presented here. Subsequent chapters focus in detail on phases and sub-phases. Figure 1-1 illustrates the flow of process consultation.

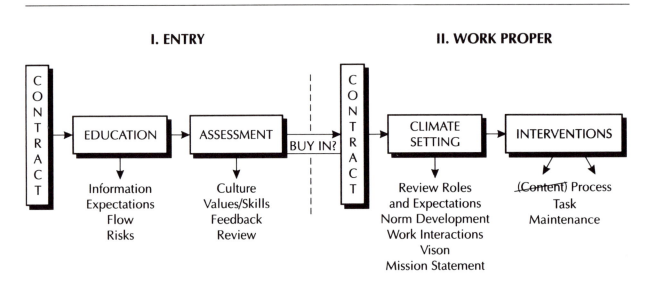

Figure 1-1. The Flow of Group Process Consultation

## Overview

This model is intended as a guide and to help the reader compare and contrast his or her own approach. What may work for one consultant in his or her organization or group may not work for another. The process recommended contains two phases, *entry* and the *work proper*.

Typically, the group process consultant meets with a manager, a person appointed by the group, or someone external to the group (e.g., the VP of HRD, the personnel director, or the director of OD). The group in question is in some need of help or wishes to be more effective, as we saw in the three scenarios at the beginning of this chapter. Process consultation is explained and a second meeting arranged with the *entire* group.

At this *education* meeting the consultant again explains the concept and flow, and what he or she can do and cannot do. If appropriate, the consultant recommends an assessment of the "state of the group." If there is agreement between the group and the consultant, a contract is made for an assessment phase. At its conclusion the consultant feeds back the data with recommendations for further work. If the consultant recommends process consultation and the client agrees, a second, preferably written, contract is drawn up and signed by the group members.

When phase II, the *work proper,* is entered, the consultant begins by helping the group clarify its values, vision, and mission (purpose). Positive behavioral norms are discussed and fixed; that is, the effective behaviors, which the group members are to reinforce, and those ineffective behaviors, which are to be reduced or extinguished. The group then works on its tasks and the group process consultant intervenes whenever he or she feels it is appropriate.

## Phase I. Entry

Phase I *(entry)* includes several steps.

### Initial Meetings

A manager or group leader usually contacts a process consultant and requests help for his or her group. Although it is appropriate that the consultant first meet with the manager, it is made clear at the outset that the *group* is the client and *not* the *manager.* The meeting with the manager is a collaborative exploration of what the problem areas are and why consultation is requested. The consultant explains group process consultation and differentiates it from other kinds of interventions. The flow of process consultation is presented with appropriate examples.

The question of fees will certainly be on the manager's agenda if not the consultant's. If the manager feels that a process consultant will be of value—and the consultant agrees—the consultant recommends a meeting with the client group. The consultant suggests that the manager speak with his or her group about their meeting and about the consultant's request to meet with the group. The major objective of the meeting between the manager and consultant is to give the manager information and understanding of group process consultation. He or she can then return to his or her group and suggest the next meeting, during which the consultant can educate group members about the process.

---

### Intervention Consideration

*Room Setup.* The room configuration itself can serve as an intervention. Group process consultants need to be sensitive to the environment in which the group works. Although they are convenient for coffee cups, tables can serve to hide and protect group members. Moreover, tables may help create a certain formality that is not conducive to creative work nor emotional expression. Flip charts, too accessible, may encourage premature scribing and promote a solution orientation versus a problem orientation. The message is for the group process consultant to be aware of his or her objectives and how the room setup can hinder or help.

---

## Education

Objectives for the client-consultant meeting are the following: acquaintance, information, behavioral examples, informal assessment, rapport, *goodness-of-fit*, and a contract to conduct an assessment.

The meeting needs to be frank and open, although in many groups the organizational culture will work against these conditions. The manager and consultant decide whether the manager should be present at the meeting with group members. If at all possible, the manager attends. If the situation is such that the members will not speak candidly while the manger is present, then the consultant may meet alone with members. This is itself diagnostic, however, and regarded as a symptom of the health of the group. A contract only for an assessment phase is recommended. This gives the consultant, manager, and group information on which to decide on the second phase.

The question of who is client is critical. The group members must have ownership, commitment, and accountability for the process and the outcome. Moreover, they must have confidence and trust in the consultant. A contract between manager and consultant will preclude the occurrence of these conditions.

The consultant must be certain that the team has enough understanding of the entire flow to make an informed choice for the next steps—assessment and education. The contracting is presented in two steps so neither client nor consultant commits to an intervention this early in the relationship.

The assessment phase and procedures are explained. The purpose is to determine the *health* of the group, major issues and tension points, strengths, and whether process consultation is appropriate and recommended for this group. The culture of the group is discussed, as is the culture of the larger organization in which the group is embedded. Data on group members' value of task and maintenance process as well as a determination of task and maintenance process skill levels are premium.

During the *education* phase, the consultant shares information about group process consultation, what it is, what it means, and how it is conducted. Many specific behavioral examples are given. Group members must understand exactly what will take place. Figure 1-1, "The Flow of Group Process Consultation," can be shown and explained to the group.

The group process consultant shares his or her expectations and explores with *all* the group members their expectations for such an undertaking. The consultant asks group members what the potential risks are and what the chances of positive results will be.

Finally, the consultant shares his or her design for an assessment process, when he or she will gather information about the culture and norms of the group—and of the parent organization—and the current "state-of-affairs" of the group. He or she explains that these data will be shared with the group during the *assessment* phase.

*Assessment*

In the assessment phase, the process consultant gathers information about the culture, overt behavioral norms, covert behaviors, the major issues facing the group, data about the people involved, and whether group members value both working on task and interpersonal issues that may impede the group (maintenance). He or she also explores whether they have the skills to use on both task and maintenance issues. The information is gathered through individual interviews, in subgroups, from the entire group, or by individual and survey instruments.

When the consultant has gathered appropriate information, he or she feeds it back to the group for assimilation and further discussion. There is discussion until the group and the consultant are able to decide about further work. When there is buy-in from both group members and the consultant, details about the *work proper* are discussed. If there is no buy-in, a discussion concerning alternatives, such as further education and training, is needed.

*Contract*

When there is buy-in, the consultant—preferably—draws up a *written* contract outlining the steps, understandings, and agreements. Copies are made for all group members, who sign it accordingly. Samples of contracts and letters of agreement are found in Chapter Four.

## Phase II. Work Proper

The *work proper* phase is also divided into parts.

*Climate Setting*

Upon contracting, written or oral, the consultant moves into the second major phase of group process consultation, namely, *work proper*. Before settling in a role to intervene as the group works, the consultant conducts *climate setting* by exploring readiness to work, personal objectives, and concerns.

He or she reviews the consultant role and expectations and asks the group to focus on norm development around both work and interactions. The group then develops a vision; that is, the group members articulate where they see themselves at the end of their tenure. Finally, the group defines exactly their mission (purpose) and objectives.

## Interventions

As shown in Figure 1-1, the major work of the consultant is to make *process* interventions,—for both task and maintenance. *Task* is concerned with the structure and elements of getting work done; *maintenance,* with the socio-emotional aspects of the group—that is, those elements that include interpersonal relations, needs, and satisfactions. As Chapter Two discusses, it is wise for the group process consultant *not* to intervene on *content matters*, even if he or she has content knowledge. Focusing on both process and content may jeopardize one's effectiveness as group process consultant.

## WHY A PROCESS CONSULTANT IS NEEDED

Returning to our three scenarios, we can answer the question—at least generically—about why a process consultant is needed. There are several reasons for using a group process consultant in these cases. A group's effectiveness and efficiency potential is determined by members' task skills and fulfillment of socio-emotional needs. Although group members may have some skills for task accomplishment, they often "forget" those skills when entering a new group. They fear using their skills when group dynamics become intense. To have present a trained, objective observer and consultant to the process—one who understands the complexity of task and interpersonal dynamics—is to ensure group success. It is also cost effective. The group process consultant intervenes in the group to readjust direction, creatively tap the energy generated by conflict, teach problem-solving and decision-making skills, and assist in meeting members' interpersonal needs.

Dynamics are generated as soon as it is known that a group will be formed and who the participants are. Although these dynamics may be positive, they can be, and often are, negative. Histories and interactions come into play and affect group functioning. Individual problem-solving skills, group composition, personal attractions and dislikes, comfort level in dealing with conflict, creative idea generation, and action step formulation are just a few of the dynamics with which the process consultant can be of help.

## ROLE DISTINCTIONS

### Who Conducts Group Process Consultation

Although it is probably in all group members' best interest to learn process skills, only *one* person should take the role of group process consultant. Moreover, that person needs to be trained in process consultation, theory, skills, and dynamics. In addition, and perhaps most importantly, the group process consultant should *not* have any other relationship with the group with which he or she is working. The process consultant is a member of the group—albeit with a role different from that of other members—and attends some 75 percent of the group's meetings, if not all.

There is often confusion about the exact nature of the group process consultant's role. All too often the terms group process consultant, facilitator, manager, leader, and consultant are interchangeable. For distinction and clarification, Figure 1-2 illustrates various role functions. Keep in mind, however, the roles may have different names in different organization.

Membership in work groups is typically a combination of internal/external, content, and psychological factors. *Internal* membership is for those who are in the group by virtue of their knowledge and potential contribution to the result, service, or product. Their attendance and investment are expected to be high. *External* membership applies to those group members who often (although not always) have staff-versus-line function and who focus on process versus content. Attendance is "when called." Contribution is usually within specific role boundaries. For example, a group may require specific content expertise and brings in a special content authority for a few hours. That person has external membership and content membership but not psychological membership, as he or she probably would not have an intrinsic investment in the overall accomplishment and completion of the task.

We will now examine the most common roles within the work group as they relate to group process consultation.

### Manager

The manager has the legitimate authority for task completion and project results and formal control over group members. The manager's primary focus and responsibility is the content, that

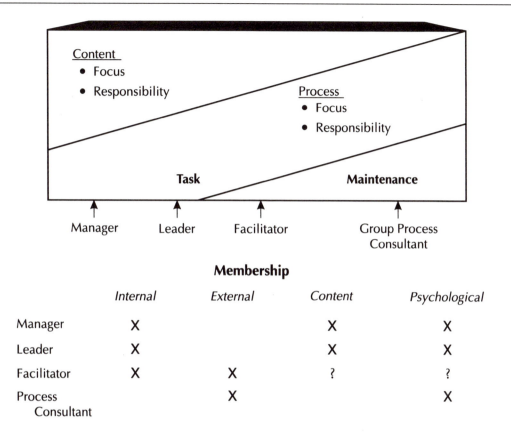

| | Content<br>• Focus<br>• Responsibility | | Process<br>• Focus<br>• Responsibility | |
| Task | | | Maintenance | |

Manager    Leader    Facilitator    Group Process<br>Consultant

## Membership

| | Internal | External | Content | Psychological |
|---|---|---|---|---|
| Manager | X | | X | X |
| Leader | X | | X | X |
| Facilitator | X | X | ? | ? |
| Process Consultant | | X | | X |

**Figure 1-2. Role Distinctions**

is, the job to be completed and/or the work to be accomplished. Although the manager may have process knowledge and skills—which are certainly helpful—he or she is in a role to get the task completed.

The manager has internal membership in the group. He or she is a regular member and has both content and psychological membership.

### Leader

The formal leader, if the group chooses to have one, is the person appointed, typically by the manager, as responsible for setting the agenda and seeing that the details around the completion of the task are monitored. Although the leader may have content knowledge, his or her expertise focuses on managing the task process. Often the leader will *conduct* the meeting or serve as scribe at the flip chart. Sometimes managers take on this role. The leader, like the manager, has internal, content, and psychological membership in the group. In some groups the manager appoints the leader to set the agenda and to manage the task operations. This role is commonly rotated from week-to-week by group members.

## Facilitator

The facilitator role is often similar to that of the leader, although the facilitator typically expects to focus on and have responsibility for some maintenance process. Indeed, the facilitator role often moves widely on the continuum in Figure 1-2, depending on the specific organization. Unlike the manager or the leader, the facilitator has the major responsibility for efficient and effective task accomplishment. Thus, the focus is on procedure and task functions. The facilitator may also comment on maintenance functions. He or she may serve as consultant to the manager, the leader, or to the group. The facilitator may or may not be present while the group is working.

The facilitator may have either internal or external membership in the group. If the facilitator is a regular member of that group or staff, he or she will have internal membership. However, if he or she is brought in from human resources, personnel, organization development, or an outside firm, the consultant will have external membership. The facilitator may or may not have content knowledge. In some organizations the facilitator has considerable content knowledge; in others, very little or none. Likewise, the facilitator, if not a regular member of the group, may not have psychological membership in the group. Although he or she will want the group to reach its objectives, the facilitator—if not a regular member of the group—may not have a high personal level of motivation for group success.

## Group Process Consultant

The process consultant is the person in role who has a contract with the group or team to sit in on *all*—or at least 75 percent of the meetings—and to make task and maintenance interventions, at various depths, into the ongoing dynamics of the group. The percent of contact time is, of course, somewhat arbitrary. It is meant to convey that the consultant's time investment is considerable if he or she is to be a part of the group's cohesion. The process consultant's aims are both task accomplishment and member satisfaction. However, *maintenance interventions are most effective when made in the service of the task.*

The group process consultant, by definition, is external to the group and has no content expertise, or at least stays out of the content. By virtue of being a regular member of the group when it meets, the group process consultant has psychological membership.

The group process consultant, as I define the role, has primary focus and major responsibility for both task and maintenance processes. In highly interdependent groups, such as high performing teams, the maintenance process is as important as the task process. The task will not be done effectively if no maintenance is done. This is problematic in organizations and groups where the expression of feelings or giving feedback are anathema.

## Manager Versus Process Consultant

The group process consultant is neither the leader nor the manager. That is, he or she does not have supervisory control nor formal power over the group members. *The process consultant refrains from entering **content** discussions.* Although a manager may have facilitative skills, he or she cannot effectively act as process consultant while in the manager role. This is also true of the staff member when called on to serve as process consultant in his or her own team. Wearing those two hats is an impossible task. This situation presents problems in organizations where the staff member, often a human resources or organization development person, acts as process consultant to his or her own group.

The distinction between the facilitator and process consultant is often difficult to make. While the process consultant is in role, he or she contracts to sit in on all group meetings and intervene at varying depths. This typically includes giving feed-back and confronting members directly about their behavior.

The facilitator may be called in for only one session or to give counsel to the manager. He or she usually does not have a contract for *ongoing* work with the team. Major distinctions, then, are in the contract between the two roles, the agreement about the nature and depth of interventions, and the amount of working time spent with the group.

One, of course, can have competence in all the roles while operating in one role per group. For example, the manager of a human resources group—while head of that unit—may be a group process consultant in another part of the company, a group leader in a second group, and a facilitator to a third. What is critical is to keep the roles separate and explicit.

A final distinction is made concerning *process interventions*. Process interventions are any attempts—by a facilitator, process consultant, leader, or manager—that aim at helping the group operate more effectively and efficiently to reach the final group objective. I use here the traditional meaning for the terms "efficient" and "effective." *Effective* relates to doing the right things; *efficient,* to doing things right. The connotation of process interventions implies that the person making the interventions is in role and is *conscious* of that role. That is, there is *intentionality* about the interventions.

Both facilitators and group process consultants can offer alternatives *and not direct* the group. Leaders can direct—when they must. Facilitation and consultation are visionary. *Direction* from a group process consultant or facilitator is a shortsighted view. A visionary view of group consultation is acquisition of task and maintenance process skills, pro-active responsibility and ac-countability for self and group. Direction and leading may be efficient but not *long-term* effective. Group members become dependent, apathetic, and unmotivated and take no ownership in the outcome or process. True group process consultation is empowering.

Moosbruker (1989) advocates a "process leader" role. The process person is "working the process" more than consulting to the process. Moosbruker lists eighteen interventions she claims appropriate for the process leader. I believe this role description grows out of a lack of understanding of the philosophical tenets of process consultation and the process leader's need to control the group and the situation. Schein (1990) decries two models that are consistent with the above, that of providing expert observation and that of playing doctor.

Moosbrucker suggests that in her experience in working with organizational groups, "...there is not time to do it for many reasons" and that the work of the process leader needs to be more *action oriented*. To fall into this trap, I believe, is to collude with the client. Groups tend to be results and task oriented and sometimes find maintenance processing nothing less than evil. However, this is exactly why group members tend not to learn skills and have difficulty finding creative solutions. It is the responsibility of the group process consultant to resist this collusion and to intervene to promote skill acquisition and a problem orientation. Thus, the view advocated here, consistent with Schein and Hackman, is long-range and not given to meeting the immediate demands of the client.

Furthermore, in my view, the role of the group process consultant *is* quite action oriented, particularly in the early stages of the group's life. The perception that the effective group process consultant is not a member of the group and instead sits back and only makes observations is inaccurate. The role of the consultant requires him or her to be *all* of the vowels: (A) assertive, (E) efficient, (I) intense (feeling), (O) organized, and (U) understanding.

It is important to make these distinctions. Role functions must be examined in each group, team, and organization. Roles will vary in definition and connotation, depending on the organization. A major problem may arise when one person tries to wear multiple hats. Situations exist in which one person attempts to carry out all four roles in working with a group; that is, manager, leader, facilitator, and group process consultant. As we might expect, it typically does not work out. Although a manager might say that he or she is "now" in role as group process consultant, the group members will not suddenly change perceptions and disregard the manager who has certain power and authority over their work life.

## SUMMARY

In summary, although I recommend a systematic group process consultation model, there is considerable freedom and choice throughout for both group members and the group process consultant. Later chapters explore each of the major phases of group process consultation, its subphases, and the techniques that help the process be effective, efficient, and satisfying to group members.

Chapter Two examines the concept of task and maintenance, the process around which the group process consultant makes his or her interventions. Now let us look again at our three sample situations.

## *Executive Planning Team* ♦ ♦ ♦

Bill, the senior manager of the executive planning group, was referred to an external consultant by the vice president of human resources. The vice president knew the consultant was skilled in group process consultation. Bill met with Scott, the consultant, and discussed his group and concerns. The consultant described what a group process consultant does, gave examples, and showed the manager the graphic, "The Flow of Group Process Consultation" (Figure 1-1). Bill found the discussion helpful and asked for a next step. Scott suggested that he next meet with the manager and the team conjointly to educate them about group process consultation. Bill agreed and then approached team members, who agreed to an initial meeting. During the meeting, the team would have an opportunity to meet the consultant, learn about group process consultation, and also see the consultant in action. The consultant, in turn, would have his first opportunity to assess firsthand how the team worked together.

## Quality Circles ◆ ◆ ◆

The human resources manager knew the company was not "ready" for quality circles and that the "leaders" would not be adequately trained in one day. She regretted not pushing back on the vice president's request for immediate implementation. She was also aware the leader-training seminar included nothing on group dynamics nor the interpersonal aspects in managing a group. The consultant explained the situation to the VP who reluctantly agreed to support additional training.

## Hospital Administration ◆ ◆ ◆

One of the few agreements the members of the hospital administrative group reached was the need for a person, external to their group, to help them manage their interpersonal issues and conflicts as they worked. A group process consultant was contacted who asked to meet with the entire group to discuss objectives, understandings, and expectations. The consultant pointed out that neither he nor the group was expected to contract until these three dimensions were clarified to everyone's satisfactions.

# Task and Maintenance Processes: Key Concepts

*I* sometimes encounter managers, group members, and consultants who have little or no idea of what group effectiveness is. Nor do they have a sense of the processes into which the dynamics of group dynamics are embedded. Chapter Two examines two key processes contributing to group success or failure, namely, *task* and *maintenance*. We also explore how process *norms* evolve and how the group process consultant intervenes on them.

## CONTENT, TASK, AND MAINTENANCE

What does the group process consultant focus on in order to be effective with the group? Chapter One discussed group effectiveness in Hackman's (1983) terms of organizational standards, member satisfaction, and the predilection of members to work over time. To help the group attain these objectives, the group process consultant focuses on two fundamental processes as the group works.

The concept of content and task/maintenance process is crucial to this understanding. The idea that there are processes operating in a group beyond the discussion of the content has been with us for a long time. Whitaker and Lieberman (1964, p. 16) state, "We assume that a subsurface level exists in all groups, but is hardest to detect in groups in which the manifest content is itself relatively coherent and internally consistent." Robert F. Bales (1950) described the task/social-emotional areas in his pioneering work on *interaction process analysis*. Edgar H. Schein (1979, 1987) articulated the concept for human relations training and process consultation.

The *content* is the work to be done, the product, the discussion elements, or the service rendered. The content is the "what," that is, the subject, problem to be solved, decision to be made, the goal, the objective.

The process, or "how," includes the approaches, procedures, rules, group dynamics, and styles of interaction. The content can be viewed as the *words;* the process, as the *music*.

The *task process,* the "how" focused on getting the group work accomplished, includes agenda setting, regulating time frames, idea-generation methods, decision-making techniques, problem-solving steps, and the testing of agreement.

The *maintenance process* is focused on getting the group's *psychosocial needs* met and the development of satisfying interpersonal relationships. The maintenance process includes membership, that is, issues of inclusion and participation, levels of influence, dealing with problem members and dysfunctional behavior, who is dominant and who is passive, and risk-taking norms.

To further understand the concept, let us take an analogous mechanical example, namely, a machine that produces dowels, small wooden rods. The product, in this case the dowels, are the *content,* the "what," the result. However, helping the dowel machine operate successfully is the *process*. That has two dimensions, task process and maintenance process.

Generically, process is "how" our dowel machine operates, its program, its strengths and limitations, and requirements to keep it operating smoothly and efficiently.

The *task process* is the "how" focused on getting the dowel produced. It includes the production methodology, the steps in the manufacturing cycle, and the time frames in reaching the completion.

The *maintenance process* is the "how" focused on the efficient running of the dowel machine. Is it overheating, or developing burrs on the roller? Is it clean and free of dirt and abrasives? Does it need oiling?

It matters little what the product service or manufactured material is. It could be a dowel, a jet engine, package delivery, or management services. Whatever the content of an operation, it has both task and maintenance functions.

Human groups are analogous to our dowel-producing machine. There exists a content and a process—task and maintenance. It is on the process—task and maintenance—that the group process consultant intervenes. Is the group operating effectively? Is the group running efficiently? Are members satisfied with what they are doing and how they are doing it?

## Executive Planning Team ♦ ♦ ♦

The executive planning team's senior manager knew the egos involved in this highly interactive and turf-protecting group. The group would be spending much time together; tensions would be high. Although task process was important—as it always is—member task skills ranged wide. Moreover, group maintenance was to be a high priority. Individual and group needs would have to be dealt with. The level of skill here was considerably less than one might expect of such a high-powered group.

## Quality Circles ♦ ♦ ♦

Two of the three quality circle leaders were very good at task process. They had learned basic procedures, agenda setting, problem solving, and decision making. They also had a good sense of when to intervene. The third leader, although having a sense of task process, was minimally skilled and very directive. In essence, he *ran* the group. Unfortunately, none were trained in maintenance process, and that is where the groups seemed to have the most trouble. They were unaware that subsurface issues could interfere with task accomplishment. Yet, maintenance issues, manifest in unexpressed feelings and suppressed conflict, were preventing the groups from focusing on and completing task. The three leaders were also fearful about their own expression of emotion in their groups and questioned its fundamental appropriateness.

## Hospital Administration ◆ ◆ ◆

The hospital administrators lacked skill in both task and maintenance processes. They lamented, "We hoped we could sit down, put our conflicts aside, and solve the problems at hand. We had no idea it could be so difficult." This naive view is not uncommon in organizations, both profit and not-for-profit.

## HOW PROCESS NORMS EVOLVE

Process norms are those consistent and enduring behaviors that group members have explicitly or implicitly agreed to. If a repeated behavior is challenged, yet continues without sanction, it is probably a norm. For example, a few members regularly arrive late for a meeting. Another member raises tardiness as an issue. After some discussion it is agreed that members should arrive on time. The very next meeting, two members are late, and although tardiness is mentioned, it does not generate much energy. Tardiness in this group is a norm.

Norms are important, because functional or dysfunctional they are the accepted behaviors by which the group will operate. The group process consultant's duty includes making norms explicit and helping the group members determine if they wish to continue the norm or replace it with another, more effective norm.

Figure 2-1 indicates that group process norms are multi-determined. Norms form from the individual members, the organizational climate in which they work, the nature of the group, and the nature of the task itself.

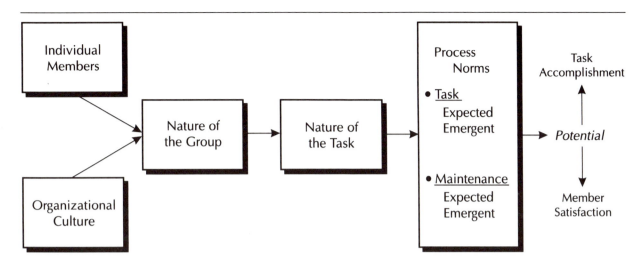

Figure 2-1. The Development of Group Process Norms

**Individual Members**

Individual group members bring their own history, personality, and life experience in solving problems and decision making. These are idiosyncratic and may not be consistent with group norms. There are personality instruments such as the Myers-Briggs Type Indicator (Myers, 1980) and the FIRO-B (Schutz, 1958) that give us a glimpse of cognitive styles and individual needs and how they contribute to the culture of the group.

**Organizational Culture**

Each organization has its own culture, which reinforces the way employees think and behave. Cultures are enduring. They are a set of common and shared understandings and meanings that hold the organization together. The culture represents patterns of beliefs that communicate the underlying values and beliefs and shape employees' behaviors.

Although the culture within divisions and departments may vary, there is a generic organizational culture that contributes to many of the behaviors exhibited in groups. For example, the organizational culture may or may not encourage openness and communication around the task or interpersonal issues. Weick (1979) uses the term *enacted environments* to describe the way in which individuals search for and develop paradigms to reduce the uncertainty of events in their lives. The organization offers a set of shared enacted environments to which the employee must accommodate for acceptance.

How we manage conflict in the organization is a function of both individual orientation and organizational culture. Is the conflict suppressed or denied? Is there an opportunity to deal with conflict "up front"? Without issue conflict, there is little hope for creative solutions.

What is the organization's problem-solving orientation? Is it focused on first exploring the boundaries and parameters of the problem, or is it solution focused? In the latter case, members leap toward premature solutions, are task oriented, and ignore maintenance issues.

Lastly, does the organization value task and maintenance processes? Do members have skills in these areas? Typically, organizations value task, whether members have process skills or not, and ignore or downplay maintenance issues.

## Nature of the Group

The nature of the group plays a role in the formation of norms. The structure of the group may be intact; that is, the group may have a relatively long life, or it may be an ad hoc group created to work on a specific task and has a brief life.

Size is also important. The larger the group, the more difficult it is to get work accomplished, although the potential is there (Kreeger, 1975). Moreover, as group size exceeds about twelve members, attaining consensus decreases dramatically. "Social loafing" (Latane, Williams, & Harkins, 1979) can occur. It becomes easier for group members to "drop out" and not contribute to group effectiveness. Kerr (1989) reports there is less satisfaction expressed by people in large groups. Members participate less often and are less likely to cooperate.

What is the composition of the group? Is it homogeneous or heterogeneous in skills and cognitive styles? What are the organizational levels of the group members? Are managers sitting in with their supervisees? Are managers or executives even represented? What is the attraction for belonging to this group? Is it voluntary or nonvoluntary? Is there prestige in being a member of this group?

All the above factors contribute to the nature of the group. The group process consultant must examine these dynamics as group norms develop.

## The Nature of the Task

We must know whether the task on which the group is working has a high priority for the organization. Are the objectives and subtasks relatively simple or quite complex? How much ambiguity is inherent in the major objectives? Will there be optimal time for task completion, or are unrealistic time schedules set? What are the intrinsic rewards available to the group members and what are the extrinsic rewards, if any? Are resources available to help the group attain its objectives, such as money, typing, and duplication?

## Process Norms

Task norms and maintenance norms are of two types. *Expected* norms are determined and predicted by the dimensions outlined above. We know, for example, if a group has tight time limits in which to complete its goal, it is likely there will be minimal strategic analysis (Gersick, 1988). Maintenance is ignored. The group becomes highly task oriented.

In addition, there are *emergent* task and maintenance norms that are specific and idiosyncratic to the group and usually unpredictable. It is this group uniqueness at which we marvel and wish we could predict. However, human behavior is complex and dynamic. I do not believe consultants will ever be able to predict the subtleties and nuances of any group.

With the development of the task and maintenance norms, expected and emergent, the group has a potential for both accomplishing its task and member satisfaction. If the norms are such that they inhibit task accomplishment and member satisfaction, the potential probability for effectiveness is diminished. If the group process consultant can help the group manage task and maintenance issues, then the probability of success and satisfaction increases.

## THE WORK OF THE PROCESS CONSULTANT: 70/15/15 RULE

The process consultant intervenes on the task process and the maintenance process. *He or she needs to consider the negative impact of intervening on the content.* As Chapter One discussed, to intervene on the content is to violate role boundaries. It is difficult if not impossible to focus on content and yet remain objective to the task and maintenance processes.

During the *work proper* phase of the process consultation flow, the consultant, given he or she has the appropriate contract, intervenes in the group *as the members work*, moving back and forth between task and maintenance. The consultant intervenes only to help the group move ahead and for member satisfaction in reaching goals. As we have discussed, a metagoal is long-term acquisition of process skills. Over time, group members themselves learn to process as issues arise or as disruptive behaviors inhibit group functioning.

On hearing about process consultation, managers sometime respond, "We'll never get any work done with all this processing." Indeed, in the early stages of the group's life, the process consultant typically intervenes more frequently than later in the group's life. Initially processing takes time. First, group members typically have not experienced group process interventions nor have they acquired the skills. Second, during the early stages of group life, there are many decisions to be made: agenda, roles, and procedures that demand the consultant to be more active.

Moreover, the early stages give the consultant an opportunity to model making interventions and delivering feedback.

*Theoretically*, there needs to be a balance between content discussion and task and maintenance focus, with about 70 percent content, 15 percent task process, and 15 percent maintenance process over the life of the group (see Figure 2-2).

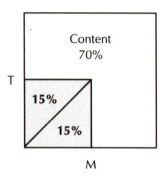

**Figure 2-2. Balance Between Content Discussion and Task and Maintenance Focus**

During the early stages of the group's life, the balance is likely to be 50 percent content, 35 percent task, and 15 percent maintenance. As members become familiar with one another and the parameters of the objectives, the balance shifts to 50 percent content, 15 percent task, and 35 percent maintenance. As skills are learned, relationships worked, decisions made, and problems solved, the balance settles to 70/15/15. Figure 2-2 shows the *optimal* balance. A 70/15/15 balance is consistent with project effectiveness, task efficiency, and member satisfaction.

Too much or too little of either task or maintenance can be disruptive. For example, as Figure 2-3 shows, an overfocus on task and an underfocus on maintenance (*task at all costs*) is like a train out of control, moving headlong to task *solution* without members ever exploring the exact nature of the problem nor checking how people feel about the task.

Conversely, low task and high maintenance (Figure 2-4) typically means that the group is more interested in its own emotional satisfaction than effectively completing the task.

When there is little or no task or maintenance processing, (Figure 2-5) and the focus is content only, the group becomes bogged down, apathetic, or bored. There may be no explicit goal, procedures, agenda, or other task processes. Abstract discussions are common as "war stories."

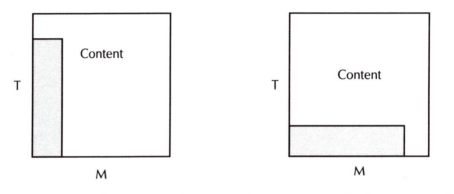

**Figure 2-3. Overfocus on Task; Underfocus on Maintenance**

**Figure 2-4. Underfocus on Task; Overfocus on Maintenance**

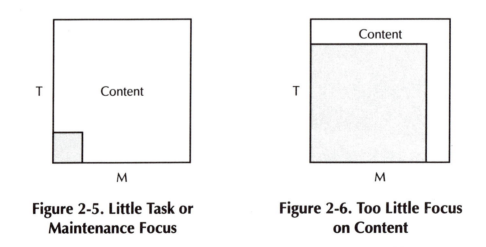

**Figure 2-5. Little Task or Maintenance Focus**

**Figure 2-6. Too Little Focus on Content**

The other extreme is high process at the expense of content (Figure 2-6). The group knows "how" to proceed and focuses on its relationships. It spends its time on process with the result that goals are not reached.

Keep in mind these percentages are abstractions and are *rules of thumb* for the group process practitioner. The important message is there must be a balance of task, maintenance, and content. Overfocus or underfocus on any component can seriously impair the functioning of the group.

## Executive Planning Team ♦ ♦ ♦

At this point, the executive planning team has not yet met, so we have no specific data about task/maintenance/content balance. Given the information we do have, however, suggests the pattern seen in Figure 2-5 will emerge. That is, ignore task and maintenance process; only content will be important.

## Quality Circles ♦ ♦ ♦

The quality circle groups are consistent with Figure 2-3, an overfocus on task and an underfocus on maintenance. There is evidence of conflict and unexpressed feelings not being dealt with.

## Hospital Administration ♦ ♦ ♦

The hospital administration group has skills around procedures and task process. Yet, they continue to spend an inordinate amount of time on maintenance. Individual needs have been put above group needs. The administrative group's balance is consistent with Figure 2-6 in which content is sacrificed for process.

**Maintaining the Right Balance**

The group process consultant moves back and forth between task process and maintenance process as the group works on content. He or she intervenes while the group is working. The content is set aside while the members deal with the process issues at hand. After an issue or concern has been worked appropriately, the group returns to content discussions. It is a dynamic multileveled process constantly shifting and moving.

It often takes time for the inexperienced group member to adapt to the process. Results- and task-oriented group members have difficulty with the maintenance process interventions. The dynamics-oriented members lose patience with the task focus. In time, as the process norms develop, the group becomes fluid. Rather than time lost to processing, time is saved by the process skills of both group consultant and members themselves.

Figure 2-7 illustrates the shifting between task process and maintenance process as the group works. While the figure is illustrative, the task and maintenance areas represented are typical. An overview is presented here, and subsequent chapters deal with the specifics.

The consultant first contracts around his or her role and checks to determine how members feel about being in the group, focusing on this particular charge, job, or task. It is not unusual that group members are "volunteered" to work on committees and task groups and really do not wish to be there. Members need an opportunity to discuss their membership and feelings about it. Although they may not be able to leave the group, the opportunity to vent their dissatisfaction has saved many a project.

It is helpful to identify other roles and establish member rotation. For example, these might include scribe or timekeeper. For the group process consultant to have an intervention frame of reference, the task is clarified. What is the charge to the group? From whom does it come? What are the evaluation criteria involved? Are there deadlines? Is a report expected, and to whom?

The group is more effective and moves faster when members create a vision, that is, a statement of values and behaviors that will drive their efforts. We tend to think of visions as created by elite groups for entire corporations. Although this situation is common, visions created by small groups can be even more inspiring and empowering. They also give the group process consultant additional behavior expectations around which to make

**Process Areas**

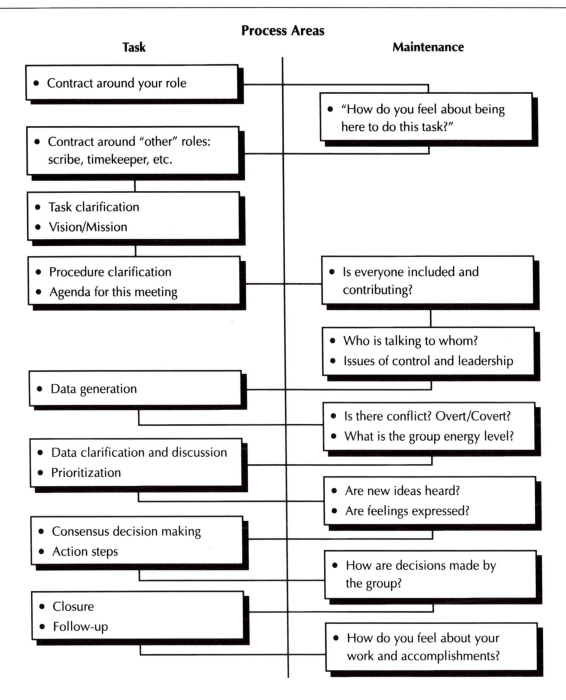

| Task | Maintenance |
|---|---|
| • Contract around your role | |
| | • "How do you feel about being here to do this task?" |
| • Contract around "other" roles: scribe, timekeeper, etc. | |
| • Task clarification<br>• Vision/Mission | |
| • Procedure clarification<br>• Agenda for this meeting | • Is everyone included and contributing? |
| | • Who is talking to whom?<br>• Issues of control and leadership |
| • Data generation | |
| | • Is there conflict? Overt/Covert?<br>• What is the group energy level? |
| • Data clarification and discussion<br>• Prioritization | |
| | • Are new ideas heard?<br>• Are feelings expressed? |
| • Consensus decision making<br>• Action steps | |
| | • How are decisions made by the group? |
| • Closure<br>• Follow-up | |
| | • How do you feel about your work and accomplishments? |

**Figure 2-7. Task and Maintenance Flow**

interventions. Likewise, agreeing specifically on the *purpose* of the group—its mission—prevents later ambiguity, confusion, and frustration.

---

### Intervention Consideration

*Unraveling the Intervention.* Many a fine intervention is undone when the group process consultant continues to talk beyond the effective point. Interventions should be short and to the point. The more the consultant talks, the greater the probability of unraveling the intervention. If you have to explain an intervention, it probably was not well formed to begin with.

"Jack, your interrupting sometimes has the effect of closing down the group." That intervention was concise and direct. However, if the group process consultant continues, "I know when I'm on the receiving end, I feel overwhelmed; and I've seen that happen here a few times. You might want to check that out. Maybe it's because you don't feel like you have a chance to have your comments heard, or maybe the group is simply moving too fast for you. I know for me it sometimes does...," the effective intervention begins to unravel.

Therefore, keep interventions short and lean.

---

When the group has these dimensions in place, it is usually appropriate to clarify the meeting agenda and how the group can most effectively proceed. Understand, these discussions will take time, generate conflict, and may surface dysfunctional behaviors. However, it is time well spent. If these issues are not dealt with, they will come back to haunt the group and will be more disruptive than at the beginning of the group's life.

The consultant's role here is to suggest, offer alternatives, and test for agreement. He or she should not direct or lead the group, because—although they might comply—the group members would not acquire the skills for their own effectiveness.

These early interventions are typically task process. By now the group is focused on the work to be done. Interactions, tensions, and overt and covert issues have increased. The group process consultant will increase the number of maintenance interventions around inclusions, communication, influence and power, leadership, and conflict. During this time the group is generating work data and may need assistance with clarification and prioritization. On the maintenance side, are new ideas heard? Are feelings expressed? On the task side, is the group working in a consensus decision-making mode? Indeed, how are decisions made? What is the most effective mode for this group?

The group process consultant continues working in this fashion with the group members making more interventions of their own over time. Finally, the group nears completion of its work. The group process consultant may intervene around final tasks to be done and how group members feel about their work and accomplishments.

The process of group consultation is difficult and exacting, and the fabric of the group life and energy is woven of task and maintenance dynamics and interventions.

Chapter Three discusses the *entry phase* in the flow of group process consultation and examines its three components: contract, education, and assessment.

# The Flow of Group Process Consultation: Phase I, Entry

*This* chapter details the first phase of group process consultation, *entry*. Chapter Four examines the second phase, *work proper*. The flow of group process consultation contains components that some readers will find familiar. Other components or their juxtaposition may be unfamiliar. Figure 3-1 (first introduced in Chapter One as Figure 1-1) is repeated here for reader convenience.

The intent is not to "sell" the model to the reader. Rather, I invite the reader to explore the model and select what "fits" his or her practices in a particular organization or group. When the opportunity arises, I recommend the reader use the model in its entirety to see what works and what does not work for him or her.

## ENTRY

In the present model, entry has three major components: *contract*, *education*, and *assessment*. We will explore each in sequence.

43

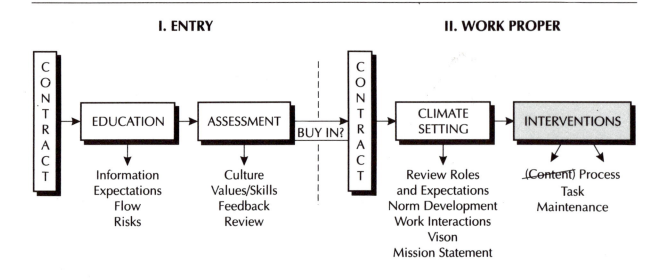

**I. ENTRY**            **II. WORK PROPER**

CONTRACT → EDUCATION → ASSESSMENT → BUY IN? → CONTRACT → CLIMATE SETTING → INTERVENTIONS

EDUCATION
Information
Expectations
Flow
Risks

ASSESSMENT
Culture
Values/Skills
Feedback
Review

CLIMATE SETTING
Review Roles
and Expectations
Norm Development
Work Interactions
Vison
Mission Statement

INTERVENTIONS
(Content) Process
Task
Maintenance

**Figure 3-1. The Flow of Group Process Consultation**

Although consultants acknowledge the importance of the entry phase in consultation, it is probably the most neglected. Yet, it is critical to the success of any consultation. Unfortunately, consultants want to get on with the *work proper*. Somehow, entry requires too much time, is not dynamic enough; or is experienced as insignificant. The hope in this chapter is to leave the reader with an understanding of the importance of the entry phase. This chapter presents specific techniques for working through entry. Without a successful entry, there rarely is a successful work proper. Entry begins with a well-defined contract.

## CONTRACTING

Contracting is the *sine qua non* of successful consultation. Without an adequate contract, the consultant can expect to be haunted by ambiguity, questions as to who really is the client, vague objectives, participant concerns about interventions, legitimacy regarding the expression of emotions, missed expectations, and disputes over time lines. Diane Kellogg (1984) lists a clear and limited contract among the nine most important characteristics in her study of successful consultations.

The importance of contracting moved Peter Block (1981) to write:

> I believe the point of maximum leverage for the consultant is probably during the contracting phase of the project. There are possibilities for impact that may be lost for the life of the project if they are not pursued in contracting. The contract sets the tone for the project, and it is much easier to negotiate a new, initial contract that to renegotiate an old one. Anyone who has been married more than a year understands this. (p. 42)

Just what is this contract or agreement between consultant and client? We will first explore the nature of the contract, the components of an effective contract, and the various kinds of useable contracts. We will then examine the decision points where a contract is advisable if not essential.

## The Nature of the Contract

The contract between consultant and client is not meant to be a legal binding document. Rather, it is a psychological and social agreement that makes *explicit* the understandings and the collaborative arrangements regarding how both the consultant and the client are expected to work together. For those, however, who are interested in the *legal* aspects of contracting, McGonagle (1982) has produced a set of specific guidelines designed to reduce the legal and ethical problems that might arise from inadequate contracts. The author offers twelve contract areas from *terms* to *termination*.

An intervention itself, a contract is created for *education* and *assessment*. The rationale is multiple. The client and the consultant need an opportunity to become acquainted. The consultant has the task of educating the client about group process consultation. He or she then needs to assess the functioning of the group. The client and the consultant can choose to continue or discontinue the consultation at any point during entry. In practice, discontinuing the consultation during entry is rather unusual. However, the consultant may recommend prior training for the client before the unit contracts for group process consultation. Clients may decide, after learning more about group process consultation, it is not what they want or need. In this model, neither the client nor the consultant agrees prematurely to a long-range commitment.

Can the consultant say "no" if he or she feels the client is not ready for process consultation? The experienced external consultant secure in his or her practice finds it easier to be objective. He or she does refuse contracts and knows when the consultation will be unsuccessful. For external consultants new to the field, or whose practice is more tenuous, refusing a contract is potentially saying no to a needed income source. If one's ego and income is on the line, refusal is more difficult.

## Contracts by Internal Consultants

Internal consultants face a different set of problems. They are often told with which group to work. Regardless of what the assessment reveals, the internal consultant does not feel the freedom to refuse. Both internal and external consultants, however, often collude in the contract phase.

For example, everyone tells the consultant how to do his or her job. The manager tells what is wrong with his or her group and how the consultant should "fix" it. The vice president calls to assign the human resources person to a group with no option but to "make something happen." The engineer tells the consultant how to manage a particular situation. Everyone is an expert on human relations, psychology, and human resource development. Moreover, as practitioners, we may not push back often enough nor present ourselves as professionally as we might. Internal and external consultants must learn to assert their professionalism. We can learn to say, "No, I don't think it is in your best interest to proceed this way. Here are the reasons why.... Let's explore alternative approaches...."

The position of the internal consultant is often tenuous. Human resource development people are sometimes seen as primarily asking questions and not giving answers. They can be told what to do with whom and when. They may not resist even when the data tell them they are moving into a failure situation. Finally, they may be expendable to the organization, last hired, first removed. We must make better and more assertive choices within our own profession if we are to be regarded with respect and professionalism.

## Contracting in the Flow of Process Consultation

There are three points in the flow of process consultation (Figure 3-1) where it is appropriate to formally collaborate on a contract:

1. After discussion with the manager and/or group regarding the education and assessment phases;

2. Following the education and assessment phases and focusing on work proper; and

3. Before each group session.

It is helpful to both client and consultant for the first contract to be oral if not written; the second is more powerful when written; the third, before a group session, is oral. The advantage of a written contract is that in addition to clarifying expectations and roles, it represents the consultant as professional and credible. As discussed, credibility is sometimes tenuous among internal consultants and human resource personnel.

At point one, it is likely that the consultant has been called in by the manager. However, as a rule of thumb, it is *preferable* to secure a contract with the *entire* group. It is critical that the consultant views the *group as client* and *not* the manager as the client. When the manager is client the consultant risks the perception by group members that he or she has a special relationship with the manager. This perception negates the establishment of trust between consultant and members and reduces the consultant's credibility.

A majority of group process consultations may fail because group or team members have little or no idea of process consultation, have few task and/or maintenance skills, and most important, see little value in maintenance, although they may value task and goal accomplishment.

Indeed, many, particularly internal, consultants downplay the importance of maintenance in the consultative process. Sometimes this attitude is related to an organizational culture that conveys "personal feelings have no place in the work setting." Sometimes it is the consultant who has difficulty in dealing with emotion and in confronting conflict. Yet, much of the energy of any group lies in its socioemotional life, which cannot be ignored, particularly if a major objective is to produce a high performance group or team. Groups and teams that must have high interactions for problem solving and that draw on the resources of all its members in synergistic fashion must have an equal balance of task and maintenance processes if they are to be successful.

The initial contract states that the consultant will conduct an *education* piece for the group, followed by an *assessment* component. The education segment will introduce the consultant to the group and the group to the consultant and will give each the opportunity to see each other "in action." It will make explicit who the client is, establish the consultant's professional credibility, and set forth a collaborative understanding as to what is expected to transpire.

At this juncture, the agreement is limited to "Phase I: Entry," with its subphases of *education* and *assessment.* Contracting in process consultation is step-wise, permitting both consultant and client choices at critical points during the process. The client can proceed at its own pace, and the process does not move on without client understanding and commitment. The second contract, usually written, and the oral contract are presented in this chapter after the following discussions on the subentry phases of education and assessment.

## EDUCATION

Essentially, the client meets with the group and explains to members what process consultation entails. If the consultant has not yet met with the entire group, the meeting also serves that purpose. It is a first opportunity for the client to meet the consultant and for the consultant to meet the group. This initial meeting may determine whether a contract is in the offering or not. The first impression made by the consultant is critical. It is imperative that the consultant *model* his or her philosophy. In current parlance, "Walk your talk."

The group process consultant presents "The Flow of Group Process Consultation" chart and describes in detail—conceptually and behaviorally—what will transpire over the course of the consultation. Numerous concrete examples are in order and usually very helpful in bringing the client to understand the process. The concept of task and maintenance balance is very important, and the consultant should leave the meeting only when this is understood by the client. The client is encouraged to raise as many questions as necessary.

A *risk assessment* can be conducted simply by the consultant's question: "What risks do you see, if any, in using a group process consultant?" Typical responses range from "Nobody ever expresses any 'feelings' in here" to "Hey, if I tell people where I'm coming from, the manager is gonna get me for it." Discussing risk allays fears, models openness, and helps to establish psychological safety for the client. In addition, consultant credibility is enhanced.

One way to improve the HRD image and credibility is to educate the client. This first meeting brings together client and consultant. The objective is to establish rapport. In addition, the consultant uses the opportunity to inform the client, exactly and behaviorally, what group process consultation is. "The Flow of Group Process Consultation" (Figure 3-1) is shown and explained, and questions are answered.

### Sharing Expectations

The group process consultant shares what (behavior and commitment) he or she expects of the client group. He or she explores what the client might expect of the consultant. Consultant expectations include what value the client places on task process and maintenance process. The consultant defines an "intervention" and gives examples. He or she points out that the members are not expected to accept *every* intervention. However, members are expected to weigh interventions carefully before rejecting them.

Often, group members have hidden fears, anxieties, and concerns about interventions. They fantasize that they might be forced into self-disclosure, confrontation, conflict, or simply the expression of feelings. The consultant, during the education phase, asks directly what the concerns and risks are in undertaking process consultation. Potential clients need to know what actually takes place during the process. They can then determine for themselves what the potential risks and disruptions are. Just posing the question of perceived risk and revealing the willingness to explore it are usually enough to quell fear, fantasy, and anxiety.

The education part is most effective when all group members are present and the meeting is held in an informal setting. This situation encourages dialogue, exchange, and interaction among the members as well as with the consultant. While the consultant is educating members about group process consultation, he or she is also gathering information about the functioning of the group: Who talks to whom; who influences whom; what form of leadership is used; the dominant patterns of communication; and the behavioral norms regarding conflict, openness, and challenge.

The consultant can expect to leave the meeting with valid behavioral data about the functioning of the group and which areas need to be further examined. The client should now have a good sense of what group process consultation is and behaviorally how the consultant will operate and conduct himself or herself.

## Discussing Assessments

Finally, the consultant discusses methods for formally assessing the functioning and health of the group. The agreement between client and consultant is that the latter will collect data about the group members and the functioning of the group. The information will be fed back to the group in a described format. The client must understand both the rationale for and the procedures involved in the assessment phase.

During the meeting the planning team had an opportunity to experience the group process consultant in action. The group process consultant obtained an initial assessment of how the group functions.

---

### Intervention Consideration

*Wording Interventions.* Often, group process consultants have a handle on the group dynamics, task and maintenance, but simply do not know how to phrase them. Like everything else, phrasing of interventions takes time, experience, and practice. Following is a selected list of intervention "stems"; practice using them, and build them into your repertoire.

"Sometimes when a person [describe behavior]..., they are really saying..."

"I am not sure about this, but let me try it out on the group..."

"Here is an alternative explanation you might want to consider..."

"Let me describe a pattern I've been observing here..."

"If I were you, I guess I would feel..."

"Let's stop for a moment and look at what's going on here..."

"Let me try this one on you..."

"I'd like to offer this observation..."

"I think that..."

"I feel that..."

"It strikes me that..."

"A pattern I have observed here is [describe]..."

"I am going to paint a picture of what I see going on here and would like your reaction to it..."

"What I am experiencing right now is..."

"I have a hunch..."

"It's time to up the ante; I suggest you try the following..."

---

**ASSESSMENT**

During the initial meeting with the group, the assessment phase of the flow is also explained. The assessment phase, of course, will differ from consultant to consultant and from one client to another. This phase is designed to gather valid data about the functioning of the group, members' perceptions, areas of tension, major issues, goals, and interpersonal interactions. The client needs to know whether the assessment involves interviews and paper and pencil instruments and the how, when, and where procedures.

Anonymity, but not confidentiality, is the guideline. That is, data will be grouped and/or summarized and fed back to the group but not with names or identification attached.

It is helpful to share with group members the questions that will be asked in the interview. The consultant might also inquire, "What other questions should I ask?" In this way, the client is collaboratively involved in the assessment process.

Diagnostic measurements are not detailed in this book, but useful instruments include the following: "Team Orientation and Behavior Inventory (TOBI)"—available from Pfeiffer & Company in San Diego, California; "Myers-Briggs Type Indicator (MBTI)," "Fundamental Interpersonal Relations Orientation—Behavior (FIRO-B)," "Work Environment Scale (WES)," and "Group Environment Scale (GES)"—all available from Consulting Psychologists Press in Palo Alto, California; and the "Group Styles Inventory (GSI)"—available from Human Synergistics in Plymouth, Michigan. In addition, there are any one of a hundred brief surveys that ask the group member to report on specific group issues.

The assessment phase may be less important for the information and data collected than for the opportunity for the consultant and client to interact around major issues and concerns. Also important is the development of a *common* data base by the client.

## Data Gathering

Information can be gathered in two major ways: individually or with the whole group. Traditionally, the consultant interviews each member of the group separately. The interview can be open ended, quasi structured, or structured. Typical areas explored are the following:

- Present issues
- Leadership

- Decision making
- Problem solving
- Tension points
- Disruptive members
- Organization and group culture
- Communication
- Work norms
- Meeting efficiency
- Conflict management
- Unit interface
- Interpersonal relationships
- Vision, mission, objectives

The *open-ended* interview is most effective when handled as an informal conversation. The consultant moves the discussion to areas of importance as he or she or the group member feels appropriate. Different questions are explored with each group member.

In the *quasi-structured* interview, the consultant asks each member to discuss the same general areas plus specific areas of importance to the client.

The *structured* interview presents each group member with the same questions, which are asked in the same format.

In addition to the interview, group members might be asked to complete a *survey* or *questionnaire* about the functioning of the group. The survey is developed by the consultant, or he or she can rely on one of many published questionnaires. If developed by the consultant, it is wise for him or her to ask a subset of members, "What questions should I ask group members?" This reduces consultant bias and promotes group ownership of the data.

If the consultant selects a published survey or questionnaire, he or she may wish to check on its validity and reliability. The ability. The majority of instruments on the market have virtually no validity nor reliability research to substantiate their claims.

Published instruments that have solid data bases permit comparison of group results with normative data. This enables group members to compare their results with samples of others who have completed the instruments. Because many of our client systems are "data oriented," these norms can be very helpful in building consultant and professional credibility.

## Perceived Value and Skills

Of particular interest is the group process consultant's assessment of member-perceived value and skills in task process and maintenance process. Chapter Two asserted that task and maintenance processes were vital to successful consultation. Group members often value task process even if they have few skills.

The maintenance process is another matter. It is not unusual to find group members who do not value the maintenance process, let alone possess skills. The above-mentioned instrument entitled "Team Orientation and Behavior Inventory (TOBI)," created by Goodstein, Cooke, and Goodstein (1983), measures a person's value and perceived skill for the task and the maintenance processes. Member scores are averaged, permitting a group score. Both individual and group scores are located on a graph.

If group scores are low for the value of task or maintenance process, additional education may be needed. If levels are low in the skills area, training may be helpful before the group embarks on group process help. All too often groups plunge into a course of process consultation before they are ready. TOBI is helpful in making that determination.

The following example illustrates the usefulness of instruments:

The TOBI was administered to a group whose members had indicated an interest in group process consultation. The members agreed that they were open to both task and maintenance interventions. The group results can be seen in Figure 3-2.

The group mean scores show a high value in task and moderate skill. However, contrary to group members' statements, the results also show both low value and low skill in the maintenance process.

The consultant fed back these data to the group with a recommendation to postpone group process consultation. Instead the consultant suggested training modules around the maintenance process including conceptual information, the value of feelings in the work setting, giving and receiving feedback, generating creative conflict, and managing spontaneous conflict. The data presentation and recommendations opened a much needed discussion about the norms and behavior of this group.

The group members accepted the recommendation for training and set up a series of modules with their HRD de-

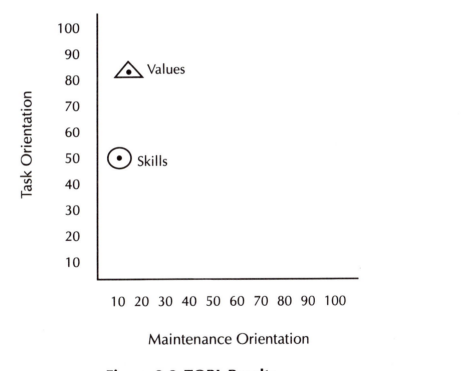

**Figure 3-2 TOBI Results**

partment. Two months later, the group was ready for and received group process consultation.

## Culture

Another area of interest to the consultant is *culture* (Deal & Kennedy, 1982; Ott, 1989; Schein, 1985). Although there are many definitions of culture, they are consistent in several ways. They convey a set of common and shared values, beliefs, expectations, and behaviors among group members. These beliefs may be implicit. If cultural norms are violated, there is typically a reaction or punishment to bring the transgressor back in line.

Each organization has its own culture. Likewise, each group has its culture, usually consistent with the larger organization. Often the culture supports behaviors that are inconsistent with effective work. Many organizations and groups have cultural norms of closed communications, avoidance of conflict, and suppression of feelings. When the group process consultant suggests a different set of norms, there is often a negative reaction and resistance.

## Feedback Session

### Summary of Individual Data

Typically, after the data are collected, the consultant groups or summarizes what he or she has found and feeds the information back to the group. It is presented anonymously but not confidentially. That is, information, issues, and concerns are reported to the group but names and identities are withheld. Group members raise questions and discuss what they have heard. Rarely are there surprises. After all, these are the issues and concerns group members have been talking about for some time. Of course, these discussions have not been in the open. Instead, the issues have been talked about in hallways, rest rooms, and behind closed office doors. Indeed, it is probably wise for the consultant about to collect data to indicate to the group there probably will not be any surprises. Many a consultant has been confronted with "We already knew this; I thought you were going to tell us something we didn't know."

The assessment approach described above is the standard, conventional, and traditional way of collecting data. There are some inherent problems, however (Reddy & Phillips, 1992).

First, a characteristic espoused in the group process consultation model is *openness*. The traditional assessment model is one of *secrecy*. That is, the consultant privately interviews or surveys individuals, summarizes the information, and feeds it back anonymously. The consultant is the primary conduit of information. Group members do not personally interact about the data. Interactions occur, if at all, *after* the data are collected. This model is consistent with what transpires in the system, a closed and conflict-avoiding process.

Second, the *consultant* determines the trends and issues. Make no mistake, what are fed back to the client are data seen through the perceptions, values, affect, theory, and cognitions of the consultant. I dare say, if ten different consultants interviewed the same client system, ten quite different sets of data would be reported. Some consultants focus on power; others, on decision making; and still others describe the organizational world in conflict-management political terms, and so on.

Third, the traditional methodology generates more negative than positive data. The client should not *avoid* negative data, but the traditional process of one-on-one interviews and surveys encourage a focus on problems, what is wrong, and what is needed to "fix" them. Moreover, group members do not have to take ownership for their information. It filters through the consultant. The approach is analogous to the confessional, investigative reporting, anonymous letters, and other secret forms of information gathering.

*Group-Generated Data*

Given the secrecy, the consultant bias, and the probability of a negative data dump, what alternatives are available for valid data gathering? Certainly, a clear, explicit, solid contract can help eliminate some of these issues. As an alternative, there is a relatively simple, exciting methodology that simultaneously builds a visible and common data base for the client members and the consultant.

First, all the group members need to generate the data *together*. Many of the traditional data-gathering techniques can still be used. The difference is rather than use techniques in a one-on-one format, use them in a group format. For example, group interviews can be conducted. The consultant interviews the group—or individual members publicly—or group members interview one another. Instruments are completed by group consensus. Although this may violate psychometric tenets, it certainly empowers members to talk to one another.

In another technique, each group member is given newsprint and colored markers. Members are asked to draw the group and their positions in it. The "product" is posted and each group member talks publicly about his or her drawing.

Marvin Weisbord's (1987) concept of *future conference* offers many ideas for data gathering, as do Lindaman and Lippitt (1979) and Srivastva and Cooperrider's (1990), "Appreciative Inquiry."

A manager might protest, "My people are not ready for this approach; they hardly talk to one another," or "That's too radical—too much public disclosure." The intent is not to hit the client between the eyes with a two-by-four. The objective is to bring group members together to talk publicly about themselves, their issues, their group, and its functioning. This is far less destructive than the conversations that go on behind closed doors.

Moreover, the group develops its data base together and publicly. Members must talk to one another to do this. It is a powerful intervention in itself. When designed appropriately, there is a balance of both positive and negative information shared. The group members take ownership for what they produce. Ownership leads to a commitment to work on issues and a focus on positive attributes of the group. Of course, the consultant needs to design the data-gathering session so group members can input on all critical areas of group functioning.

Finally, the group data-gathering process eliminates the need for a separate feedback session. Members have data about group functioning and whether a group process consultant is needed. If there is "buy-in," the group is ready to enter the work proper phase in the flow of process consultation.

Pitfalls are inherent in this alternative also. Group members may avoid raising issues publicly, or they may tacitly collude in avoiding anxiety-arousing interpersonal problems. In addition, the group approach requires a high level of consultant skill to manage the process and the group. The consultant needs to feel personally comfortable with whatever approach he or she applies. The message here is that there are assessment alternatives from which we can draw. We are limited only by our own paradigms, anxiety, and facility.

As part of the assessment-feedback session, the consultant recommends or does not recommend group process consultation as an intervention of choice. For example, the consultant may find that the MBTI data reveal a group of highly introverted, thinking, judging members and that there is also little value for maintenance. The consultant, in this case, may suggest some kind of interpersonal interaction training before recommending process consultation. In the case discussed earlier, TOBI data revealed a discrepancy between what group members voiced about valuing the maintenance process and what the instrument revealed. Whatever the recommendation, it must be done in an affirmative, supportive way.

## The Second Contract

If there is client "buy in" for the process consultation recommendation and consultant willingness to work with the client, a second agreement or contract is negotiated. This is most important. It outlines, in writing, what the consultant will do and list his or her expectations, intervention areas, and personal values. Group members are expected to sign off on the letter of agreement, indicating their understanding, agreement, and commitment.

The following "letter of agreement" is a sample of a written contract. The sample is generic, and the contract should be tailored to the consultant's own organization and needs. If the consultant chooses not to develop a written contract he or she might include the major dimensions in the oral discussion and agreement.

Let us now look at the elements in the sample letter of agreement.

## *Letter of Agreement for Group Process Consultation*

### Definition

Group process consultation is the reasoned and intentional interventions, by the consultant, into the *ongoing* events and dynamics of a group with the explicit purpose of helping that group effectively attain its agreed-on objectives.

### Role of the Consultant

As the group process consultant, I will be in a role with which you may not be familiar. This Letter of Agreement is presented primarily to inform you of what you can expect of me as the consultant and what is minimally required of the team/group/staff members to make this consultation effective.

I typically intervene (comment, make suggestions, etc.) in the group *while the group is working.* I comment on what I observe; how people are interacting and dealing with one another; how the group is working as a unit; and how members might be more effective. When appropriate, I will ask members how they *feel* about what has occurred. I do not intervene on the content. I see that as *your* area of expertise.

The focus of my interventions may be *how* the group is working, or how members' *behaviors* are or are not contributing to the effectiveness of the group in reaching its ultimate and stated goals and objectives.

My interventions will be in keeping with the goals that the group members have *explicitly* agreed on. Thus, one of the first areas on which I will focus will be what the group determines to be its vision, mission, and objectives.

Typical areas on which I will intervene are the following:

- communication
- problem-solving
- decision-making
- leadership
- interpersonal relations
- conflicts

These interventions might be at a group level, an interpersonal level (between a few people), or an individual level.

### My Expectations of Group Members

My primary expectation is that group members use me as an instrument and resource to help you become more effective at task accomplishment. While you may not accept my interventions as accurate, I do expect you to consider them as possibilities and alternatives.

I would also hope that issues you might have with me be brought out in the open, where all group members can work on them.

**Personal Values of the Consultant**

The client system and/or individual members have a right to know—*at any time*—my objectives and rationale for whatever I am doing or suggesting.

Members always have a choice of involving or not involving themselves in any survey, activity, simulation, or exercise that I offer.

I do not intentionally intervene at a level deeper than that which the client or participant can handle, nor will I leave the system more disrupted than when I entered, when no follow-up is planned.

Any personal information coming out of a survey, workshop, seminar, or consultation is confidential and/or anonymous and will not be shared with anyone except with the explicit permission of the person(s) involved.

I assume that people learn in different ways and rates and not by being overwhelmed or made excessively anxious.

I consider conflict and resistance to be a natural outgrowth of the differences and interactions between people and not inherently negative nor destructive. Although it might not be resolved, conflict can be managed.

I construe my role as consultant/facilitator to include protecting employees, workshop participants, and organization members from personal embarrassment, scapegoating, or behaviors that I feel may be personally destructive to them, others, and/or the organization.

**Endorsement**

I understand the definition, role, and expectations set forth in this letter, and, as a team/group/staff member, I will try to fulfill the consultant's expectations of me and work toward the effective functioning of the group.

_____          _____
Consultant                                Group Member

_____          _____
Date                                      Group Member

                                          _____
                                          Group Member

                                          _____
                                          Group Member

                                          _____
                                          Group Member

| | |
|---|---|
| *Definition* | Beginning with a definition of process consultation is helpful. Most clients have neither an accurate concept of the process nor recognize that the process consultant will be focusing on both task and maintenance dynamics. Use whatever definition fits for you, but be prepared to review the exact meaning of the words contained in the definition. |
| *Role of the Consultant* | This subheading includes a description of the behaviors that can be expected from the process consultant. Include here examples of your typical interventions. Again, be prepared to give multiple examples to the client when reviewing the letter of agreement. Also included in this section are dynamic areas in which the process consultant will make interventions. |
| *My Expectations of Group Members* | All too frequently the client thinks only of how the consultant conducts himself or herself to the exclusion of member behavior. This section reminds the client that it collectively is responsible for behaviors. By describing what the consultant expects from group members, he or she is setting norms for effective behavior leading to task accomplishment. |
| *Personal Values of the Consultant* | The group process consultant enters into a relationship with a client having an implicit set of values around which he or she does his or her work. These values should be made *explicit,* so that the client understands what the consultant's values, driving forces, and assumptions are. It also helps establish a sense of psychological safety for the client to know that the consultant is operating in the best interests of the client and will protect the client accordingly. |
| *Endorsement* | Lastly, there is a definite advantage in having the client sign off on the letter of agreement. It becomes a public record, so-to-speak, and increases ownership and commitment to the process.<br><br>In summary, the more *everything* is made explicit, the fewer problems the consultant will have. The concept of the contract or letter of agreement models openness and collaboration. It builds trust between and among parties, the very fundamental components upon which an effective and successful consultation |

is built. Of course, one should not promise magic in the contract; conversely, one should not proceed unless a clearly articulated contract is in the hands of both client and consultant.

## The Oral Contract

The third point at which the process consultant can contract is immediately before the group begins its work in "Phase II: Work Proper."

When the process consultant sits with the group for the first few times he or she can orally contract around his or her role. The consultant describes again, briefly and behaviorally, what he or she will be doing and why. This oral contract serves to remind the group members of the earlier written contract and sets the stage for work. As the following sample oral contract illustrates, the approach is kept simple and leaves the opportunity open for client questions and expectations.

### The Oral Contract with a Group

Before we begin, I would like to take a few minutes to talk about how I construe my role.

I would like the freedom—at any time—to comment on what I see happening in the group around behaviors that are either facilitating or impeding the group toward its goal.

I will not intervene on the content of your work. I see that as *your* responsibility and the focus of your expertise.

The intent and hope is that over time *you* can learn to make these same interventions yourself in order to move the group along and thus become more effective.

I wish to comment whenever I feel it is appropriate. I do not ask that you necessarily accept all my interventions. I do ask that you weigh them and not reject them out of hand.

Is all this agreeable to each of you?

I would also like to know what you expect of me and to discuss whether it is something that I perceive to be within my role as process consultant.

Once again the consultant has an opportunity to present himself or herself as authoritative, credible, and maintaining clear role and work boundaries.

Chapter Four explores the *work proper* of the consultant. It looks at methods for creating an effective work climate and developing behavioral norms as guidelines. The group is first assisted in articulating its values, vision, mission, and objectives.

## Executive Planning Team ♦ ♦ ♦

During his first group meeting, the consultant, Scott, was specific and concrete as he described group process consultation and its potential. He presented the "Flow of Group Process Consultation" and gave behavioral examples. There were guarded questions and concerns raised around confrontation, time required, expression of feelings, and solving problems as a group versus individually, the latter being the current norm. Scott responded openly and urged group members to talk to each concern directly. This method was obviously difficult; each member spoke to the group as if presenting a lecture. Scott pointed out these behaviors as data in support of group process consultation. The members were impressed with the here-and-now observations and warmed to the idea of retaining a group process consultant.

Before the group made a final decision, Scott recommended he gather data about their individual styles, aspirations, and potential tension points. They agreed, and the following week the consultant administered a self-scoring styles instrument and took the members through a few group data-gathering activities. They prioritized interpersonal areas on which they needed to work and selected task areas they wished to approach first. There was considerable excitement generated as the group agreed to work with the group process consultant.

## Quality Circles ♦ ♦ ♦

With the additional training, which now included group dynamics and the interpersonal aspects of managing groups, two of the quality circle leaders, Kim and Michael, now felt much better prepared to deal with their groups. The third, Larry, found discomforting the challenge of exploring feelings in his group. "If we'd only stick to the task, we'd be all right," he thought. Upon returning, Kim and Michael decided to renegotiate their roles and contract. They described their training and made a case for working both task process and maintenance process.

*Circle I.* Kim's group was immediately receptive, in part because of her warmth and supportive approach. She acknowledged it would be difficult but suggested the group periodically take time to learn new skills. The first activity Kim conducted was on giving and receiving feedback. It was done well and with empathy for the somewhat anxious participants. Kim had group members first practice on scripted examples. She then moved them to real-time task issues and finally mild maintenance issues. The activity was very well received.

*Circle II.* Although Michael's group agreed to explore a new contract, members were quite tentative. Michael believed in the approach, but his style was somewhat standoffish and intellectual. However, Michael did describe his recent training and explained how he thought it could help the group. He then shared what he had been observing in the present group, being careful to describe group behavior and not to focus on individuals.

He asked group members for their reactions to his observations. A torrent of comments were unleashed—from observations about the group process, to what the group should do, to the uncomfortable chairs. Michael was a bit overwhelmed and was not sure how to manage the comments, let alone the feelings. One of the members suggested the comments be put in "categories" to be dealt with later. This was reinforced by a second member. Most of the group agreed. While Michael was deciding whether to intervene, a third member stood up and began writing at the flip chart. The meeting ended at this point, but with enthusiastic support for continuance of this new process.

*Circle III.* The third leader, Larry, simply could not buy into the idea that he should be anything but directive. He did describe his training to the group but laughed off the "feelings" idea. When one of the group members suggested it might be a good idea to be more open about their conflicts and disagreements, she was put down by other members. Larry did not intervene. He suggested an agenda for the day and the group plodded on.

## Hospital Administration ♦ ♦ ♦

The administrators met with the group process consultant, Laura, and immediately barraged her with questions about what she was *going to do*. She asked that she first have an opportunity to explain what group process consultation is and what could be expected of her in the role of group process consultant. She also wished to share what she expected of group members. Laura presented her understanding of group process consultation, responded to questions, and engaged the group in dialogue, not just with her but with one another. She emphasized that the responsibility for success rested with the group and not with her.

The staff was impressed with her clear presentation, understanding, assertiveness, and desire for collaboration. Laura interviewed the group—as a group—and gathered the information she felt necessary to proceed as a group process consultant. Her major objective was to have the group develop a shared and common data base. Laura and the group agreed on a collaborative relationship. She explained the next step would have the group articulate its mission, understand one another's roles, and create a set of behavioral working norms.

# The Flow of Group Process Consultation: Phase II, Work Proper

# 4

*We* now consider the second major phase in the flow of process consultation, *work proper.* We will look at setting a proper climate for getting work done. This includes roles and expectations, norm development, and creating a vision, mission, and set of objectives. We then consider the consultant, in role, making interventions as the group works. We examine a way of formulating when to intervene, based on what group members say versus how they behave. Finally, we will explore the maintenance and task issues that you can expect as the *work proper* phase begins.

## CLIMATE SETTING

At the end of phase one, the *entry,* the client has been educated regarding the nature of process consultation. The client agreed to an assessment and—with those data in hand—decided to use a group process consultant. The consultant is ready to sit in with the group and make interventions as the group works. It is helpful first to set a working climate for the group.

## Roles and Expectations

Although it might have been explained during the education session, the consultant reminds the group that he or she will not work at the flip chart, lead the group, nor keep time. These roles can be rotated among members. However, some group process consultants feel that as a member of the group they, too, should take their turn in the rotation. This certainly has merit and may help cement the credibility of the consultant and speed group cohesion.

In addition, the consultant makes clear that he or she will not intervene on the content—whether the consultant has content knowledge or not. As discussed earlier, for the consultant to involve himself or herself in the content is to violate role boundaries. It is helpful to remember that a major objective in group process consultation is the assimilation of skills by the client, so that members will be able to work more effectively in the future as well as in the present.

## Norm Development

In norm development, members discuss and agree on work procedures and guidelines for interaction. Explicit work procedures such as type of decision making (e.g., majority vote, consensus, consensus attempt, and quorum vote), problem-solving sequence, and data-generating methods (e.g., individual brainstorming methodologies) are valuable to the group (Gordon, 1961; VanGundy, 1981; Koberg & Bagnall, 1981; Bransford & Stein, 1984).

Work norms reduce ambiguity, offer a framework, and help the group function smoothly. Likewise, interpersonal interaction norms minimize unproductive conflict and encourage efficient discourse. They can be developed quite easily and serve as behavioral guides for more efficient interactions. Neal Clapp (1980) has written an excellent article on norm development in work groups. It is a piece worth reading.

Although there may be a formal leader, such as a manager, the leadership of the group might rotate, depending on the task, the comfort of the manager, the skill of the members, and the inclination of the group.

---

### Intervention Consideration

*Interaction Norms.* Generating interaction norms can be as simple as the consultant's asking the group members, "What behaviors make for a lousy meeting?" Members typically respond with such comments as "Interrupting somebody who is talking; being late; not contributing; not staying on track." The group process consultant then asks, "What behaviors support an effective meeting?" The items are posted on newsprint. When a consensus is reached about which items will be included, copies are posted on each side of the room. In this way, members can see the agreed-on *norms* at all times. Group members quickly learn to use the norms without the intervention of the consultant. They will observe a dysfunctional behavior, point to the chart and comment, "Number three; remember number three?" Of course, the list also makes it easier for the consultant to comment on member behavior. In a sense, the norm list legitimizes interventions in these areas.

---

## VISION, MISSION, OBJECTIVES

Any group needs to know *who* it is, *what* its purpose is, and *how* it is going to get where it intends. The vision, mission, and objectives statements—although requiring time—permit the group to make explicit these criteria. A most articulate discussion of vision, mission, and objectives can be found in Block (1987).

## Vision

Vision refers to the values that drive the group. Although values are always present in groups, they are rarely made explicit. Explicit and agreed-on values help create a more realistic and attainable vision. This vision is not the vision of the organization, although it should be consistent with that vision. The group's vision is a future statement, *written in present tense, active voice,* describing a chosen way of being and behaving. For example, a finance department originally drafted the following vision statement.

> Value will be added to the company through proactive partnership with our customers. We will focus on key objectives with responsive, timely, and efficient service.

With minor edits into present tense and active voice, we see a more powerful vision.

We add value to the company through a proactive customer partnership. We focus on key objectives with responsive, timely, and efficient service.

A self-directed team produced the following statement of values:

S_____ is simply the best team in the community of teams. We risk, create, and self-empower. We are the standard by which other teams are compared.

In each case, the statement is about what the group *is* and not what they *do* or produce. That is in the mission statement.

---

### Intervention Consideration

*Visioning.* It may help to discuss the visioning process in terms of the self-fulfilling prophecy. That is, if you can envision a future of your design, you will act accordingly and bring that vision to reality.

There are video tapes available that serve well to create the proper set and mood for visioning; for example, *Productivity and the Self-Fulfilling Prophecy: The Pygmalion Effect*, produced by CRM McGraw-Hill Films; *The Power of Vision* and *Discovering the Future: The Business of Paradigms*, both Joel Arthur Barker videos produced by Charthouse Learning Corporation.

---

The consultant can ask the group create their own values list or use a published list. A predetermined list (Beck & Hillmar, 1986) saves time in discussing what a value *is;* it is also uniform and facilitates the activity (see Figure 4-1). With a predetermined list, the consultant asks the group members individually to rank the top three values they wish to drive their group. They are also asked to select the three least desired. When individual work is completed, the group attempts, by consensus, to select three or four major value drivers. The activity is typically intense and productive as members disclose value preferences and the reasons for selection.

When the group reaches value consensus, the consultant gives an input on vision. Members are now asked to create an individual vision, keeping in mind the values discussion and consensus. As before, when the individual work is completed, the group is asked to create a *group* vision. The activity can be difficult but energizing.

A technique that helps the process is to request that each member write his or her vision on flip-chart paper, then post it. Members sit before the charts and look for commonality. They circle in red key words they would like to see in the final version.

The group can be divided into subgroups to draft vision statements. Statements are discussed. A committee (members from each subgroup) is selected to return with a draft. Copies are given to each member for final wordsmithing, comments, and revisions.

The vision statement must be one with which the group can live, as it will guide their work and group behavior. It also serves as a guide for the group process consultant's interventions.

## Mission

Clarification of the *mission* is next. Whereas the vision describes "what we are," the mission describes "what we do." What is our *purpose*? What exactly is expected of us regarding a product? What charge have we been given—and by whom? What expectations have the people who will review and evaluate our progress and our product?

It is surprisingly common that groups, teams, and committees do not take the time to clarify precisely what they are about to embark upon. Although it does take some discussion, agreement is not particularly difficult to attain.

## Objectives

Once the vision is in place and the mission set, it is time to define specific objectives. That is, given our mission, what are

What I value in organizations that I belong to is for the organization to be (please number, from highest of 1 to lowest of 19, in order of importance to you):

_____ **A. Achieving**—making a worthwhile contribution and meeting the needs of individuals.

_____ **B. Balanced**—maintaining appropriate concern for the needs of society, the organization, and individuals without discounting any of the three.

_____ **C. Beautiful**—having a sense of the aesthetic in its architecture, landscaping, and work environment.

_____ **D. Caring**—making members important and providing a place where members relate to one another well, and feel that they are wanted.

_____ **E. Comfortable**—a place where people fit easily, relate to one another well, and feel that they are wanted.

_____ **F. Egalitarian**—providing equal opportunity for all and access to information needed to control their own lives.

_____ **G. Exciting**—offering stimulating, active opportunities for members to risk, to grow, and to express themselves.

_____ **H. Free**—providing a place where members can make choices, express their independence, and participate in decisions that affect them.

_____ **I. Fulfilling**—having a sense that the work is meaningful and the organization contributes to society as the individual contributes to the organization—a place where I want to go to work.

_____ **J. Harmonious**—fostering inter- and intragroup harmony, given to solving problems rather than blaming and finding fault.

_____ **K. Humanistic**—being concerned more with contributing to human welfare and the quality of life than the competitive struggle for markets and a standard of living.

_____ **L. Integrated**—possessing unity and wholeness beyond a simple summing of the parts—the parts have a working relationship.

_____ **M. Purposeful**—having a clear sense of purpose—a mission—to which we are committed and use to evaluate all our results and activities.

_____ **N. Spontaneous**—being responsive to needs, flexible, open to change, not bound by strong traditions when they are not functional.

_____ **O. Structured**—operating by a clear set of team policies, rules, and procedures that state what is expected of members and how they should behave.

_____ **P. Supportive**—supplying the necessary resources, tools, equipment, and training to get the job done; the manager gets us what we need and encourages us.

_____ **Q. Secure**—being strong enough that I am not worrying about being laid off or fired for no fault of my own.

_____ **R. Successful**—a visible and credible organization which has a good growth and profit (service) record; well established.

_____ **S. Warm**—encouraging friendly and information relations, emphasis on enjoying fellowship.

Source: "Values I Seek In My Organization," by Richard S. Underhill in Beck, A.C., & Hillmar, E.D., Eds. (1986), *Positive Management Practices*. San Francisco, CA: Jossey-Bass. Used with permission.

## Figure 4-1. Ranking Form for Organization Values

the goals by which we know we are on the right path? How are we going to evaluate the goals?

We can expect the objectives to change over time more readily than will the mission and the vision. Keep in mind the group has not yet worked on the *content* of the task. Although the present description makes the formulation of vision, mission, and objectives appear to require much time, in practice it does not. Certainly, it requires some time, and—unfortunately—more time than some organizations are willing to invest. This is a short-sighted view but a reality in many modern North American organizations, in both the for-profit and not-for-profit sectors.

What are the task and maintenance issues of which the group process consultant must be aware during the initial stages of Phase II? It is not unusual for participants to balk at discussing values or creating a group vision. Even if you discussed values and vision during the education subphase, your attempts to implement them are likely to meet with resistance. Following is a typical dialogue:

**Mike:** Let's get to work. Why are we doing this junk?
(a group member)

**GPC:** Mike, you sound pretty annoyed and anxious to get going. I can understand that. There is a lot to do.

**Mike:** Damn right! We waste enough time around here.

**GPC:** Maybe it would help all the way around if I again went over why I think we need to do some of this stuff....

**Members:** (Silence)

**GPC:** (Humorously) Thanks for that ground swell of support.

**Members:** (Laughter)

**GPC:** Please bear with me as I go over this...but I think you'll find it helpful in the long run.

The group process consultant nondefensively and briefly re-explains what an effective group is and the concept of vision in the context of a self-fulfilling prophecy. In this case, a football team visualizing Superbowl play is used as a metaphor.

| | |
|---|---|
| **GPC:** | What do you think...? Where are you...? |
| **Members:** (except Mike) | Makes sense to me....Sounds good....Let's move on it. |
| **GPC:** | Mike, where are you? |
| **Mike:** | (laughing) Geez, you guys would talk me into anything. |
| **GPC:** | Well, where you are and how you feel is important...as it is to any of us at any time. I appreciate your raising the issue. Are we at a place we can move on? |
| **Mike:** | (nodding affirmatively) Yeh, good; let's do it. |

In this dialogue we see the group process consultant non-defensively handling whatever comes up. He acknowledges the importance of Mike's feelings and eagerness to move on; yet, establishing values and vision is also important. The consultant uses humor in requesting the group to "bear with him" as he does a brief review. The acknowledgement of Mike and asserting the importance of values and vision permit the group to move on. The consultant also takes the opportunity to reinforce the importance of pausing in the work to check out where members are and how they are feeling about their work.

## WORK PROPER

The basic work of the group now begins. The group process consultant intervenes *as the group works.* It is helpful to reiterate the oral contract (Chapter Three) to the group the first few times to remind group members of how the consultant behaves and intervenes.

No matter how sophisticated the group, if they have not previously worked with a group process consultant, initially they can find the process a bit awkward. Often, group members are familiar with a facilitator. They hold back and wait for direction. When the consultant suggests, rather than directs, there is some floundering and sometimes anger. Suggestions from the consultant may be ignored. The consultant may have to intervene on that issue itself.

Schein (1961) describes a process of unfreezing, changing, and refreezing. Although his work—its roots in Lewinian field theory (Lewin, 1951)—grew out of "brainwashing" efforts by Chinese Communists, the theory has been applied to sensitivity training groups, personal and organizational change (Schein & Bennis, 1965), and the present group process consultation model.

In the early life of the group, members find that their work attempts are not effective. Members do not listen to one another; goals are unclear; procedures are faulty; and leadership is inconsistent. The group process consultant intervenes. Members are *disconfirmed* (Schein & Bennis, 1965). In a reconfirmation attempt, members look to one another and the consultant for effective and efficient behaviors, that is, doing things right and doing the right things. Since the consultant will not direct them, the members themselves must try out the new behaviors, thus, learning the process.

The group process consultant intervenes more frequently in the early life of the group. Members are more tentative and not as willing to try out new behaviors as they are later on. Also, in the middle and later stages of the group, members have learned new skills and group-related behaviors. Stages of work group activity are explored in Chapter Six.

---

### Intervention Consideration

*Check on Member's Feelings.* Build into your contract the expectation that you will routinely (at least every half-hour) check on how group members are feeling about their work.

*Quick check:* "How do you feel about what you are doing right now?"

This small intervention pays big dividends. It will not be long before they are checking with one another.

## Intervening in the Gap

Group process consultants sometimes know the dynamic areas on which to intervene, yet ask *when* they should intervene. A focused way of moving the group is what I call *intervening in the gap*.

Argyris and Schon (1974) describe what they call "espoused theory versus theory-in-use." *Espoused theory* is the behavior we state we value and believe is a part of our interpersonal repertoire. Our espoused theory may or may not be manifest in actual behavior. Our *theory-in-use* refers to the actual behaviors in our repertoire as seen by others. In the words of Argyris and Schon:

> When someone is asked how he would behave under certain circumstances, the answer he usually gives is his espoused theory of action for that situation. This is the theory of action to which he gives allegiance and which, upon request, he communicates to others. However, the theory that actually governs his actions is his theory-in-use, which may or may not be compatible with his espoused theory; furthermore, the individual may or may not be aware of the incompatibility of the two theories. (p. 7)

Groups collectively espouse certain behaviors through vision, mission, goals, norms, and work activities. Likewise, individual group members espouse effective group behaviors. Both the group, as a group, and individual members behave in ways that may be inconsistent with those espoused behaviors. It is in this *gap* that the group process consultant intervenes. The gap may be between what an individual says and how he or she behaves or between what the individual says and what the group espouses. The gap can also be between how the member behaves and the normative behavior of the group, and so on. Figure 4-2 illustrates the areas in which gaps occur and where interventions are needed.

The group process consultant must be alert to remember various espoused behaviors. A vision, mission, goals, and norms in place, of course, make the process considerably easier. The group process consultant intervenes in the gap when he or she sees the disparity in behavior. The reader may find it helpful to

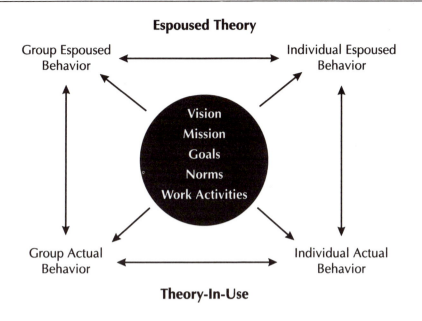

**Espoused Theory**

Group Espoused Behavior ⟷ Individual Espoused Behavior

Vision
Mission
Goals
Norms
Work Activities

Group Actual Behavior ⟷ Individual Actual Behavior

**Theory-In-Use**

**Figure 4-2. Intervening in the Gap**

use a flip chart by listing various statements heard and observed behaviors. They can be listed at appropriate points on the chart and later commented on accordingly.

Chapter Five examines the types of interventions that are available to the group process consultant.

## *Executive Planning Team* ♦ ♦ ♦

By their first regular meeting with the consultant, some of the excitement about working together had been replaced with apprehension. This increased somewhat after Scott reiterated his role through an oral contract. He restated the desirability of his intervening on both task and maintenance processes.

Scott suggested the group might decide to establish some other roles they could rotate, such as time keeper and scribe. One member, Tim, questioned, "Why can't you do that? Isn't that what we pay you for?" Scott explained, nondefensively, the value of members taking new roles, and also freeing him to focus on the group process.

Over half the group members wanted to immediately plunge into the task. Scott suggested they might first consider talking about how they felt about being there and working on the planning project. After forty seconds of silence, Harry said, "I am pretty overwhelmed with the enormity of the task." Bill attempted to tell him he shouldn't be overwhelmed. Scott intervened, intimating that it was okay to feel whatever anyone was experiencing. He then asked what other members were feeling about the planning project. This began an intense and prolonged exchange between members. It was also apparent that team members had very different views on what charge they had been given and the expected outcomes.

During the discussion, Scott observed the mediocre level of interpersonal skills. He suggested that the group take a little time to develop behavioral norms by which to work.

The session ended with an agenda for the next meeting, which included charge clarity and agreement, development of a time line, and a sense of vision; that is, how the team would describe itself looking toward the end of its tenure.

A quick feedback check (a few words each) produced: "relieved, right-on, cautious, good work, we're on our way, a lot to do, too much feeling not enough work, satisfied," and thumbs up.

## Quality Circles ♦ ♦ ♦

*Circle I.* Kim rapidly increased her confidence and her competence. Circle I flourished. Members were open and confronted the appropriate issues. Over time, however, group members began to see themselves as superior to the other two circles. In many ways they were, but their competition took on a derisive tone. In addition, competition became a major covert issue within the team. Members felt the freedom to express ideas, many of which were creative and innovative. However, ownership for one's ideas was strong; ideas were often lost in the intense competition. Kim suggested that the competitive comments about Circles II and III might be a reflection of competition within the Circle I. This was hotly denied by group members and quickly dropped. Kim chose to wait for the group to generate more data before again intervening.

*Circle II.* In Circle II, Michael felt he had unleashed a monster, yet was pleased about the reactions. He also felt some annoyance at the member who intervened about posting the comments; he was annoyed because he had not thought of it sooner. At the next meeting Michael asked if the group wanted to work on project or maintenance issues. The answer was "both." After discussion, the group agreed to work on the project and agreed that Michael intervene when he saw interpersonal issues avoided by the group. They would also leave a half-hour before the end of the session to tackle one of the maintenance issues left from the previous week.

Michael used what he had learned at the training session and worked hard at keeping the group on task and yet responding to maintenance issues. For example, he described his observation that the group continued to make decisions, although minor, when not everyone was in agreement. Cynthia commented, "Well, people should speak up when they are not in agreement." Rudy, a mild-mannered member responded, "I'm still thinking about it and the group is off and running with something else." Cliff offered, "Michael, why don't you check when you think that we may not be in agreement?" Michael felt this was a reasonable request from the group.

*Circle III.* Circle III continued to flounder. Members grumbled about wasting time, and Larry became more frustrated and punishing on his interventions. He suggested that perhaps the group needed "some new blood to help stimulate action." Fred retorted, barely audibly, "Maybe we need a new facilitator."

Rather than use the opportunity to explore members' feelings, Larry opted to move on, asking again, "Should we get some new members on this team?... Well, give it some thought and we'll pick it up next week."

## Hospital Administration ♦ ♦ ♦

At the next session Laura again described her role and how she might be of help. She then suggested that it might be of value if the group came to some understanding and agreement about their task.

**Ned:**       Look, we know why we're here; let's get on with it.

**Laura:**     You may be right, Ned; please summarize that understanding for the group.

**Ned:**       Aahh, yea, sure.

Ned then states his understanding of the task.

**Jeremy:**    Wait a minute; that's not what we're about.

**Ted:**       Jeremy's right. Our mission is to figure out the direction and future for this hospital.

**Theresa:**   Well, that's not quite accurate.

The group members, with Laura's help, spent the rest of the session specifying their charge. Members tended to wander, but Laura kept the group focused with a simple cognitive intervention: "The group may be off topic again." By the end of the session, members were pleasantly surprised they had general agreement on their mission, their primary purpose. Because of Laura's interventions, the group kept its focus and completed more work that it typically did.

Laura also suggested that the group might be better served if it developed a set of specific behavioral norms to guide its work and interactions.

# Types and Depth of Interventions

# 5

$W_e$ have a framework for making interventions and for when to make them. Questions now raised are "What *type* of interventions can I make? Should I focus my interventions on the group as a whole or on individuals? How intense should my interventions be? How deep should I go with this group?"

This chapter examines what types of interventions are available to us as group process consultants. We decide the target or focus of the intervention and how intense we intend the intervention. We determine the depth of our intervention, then look at type as a way of reaching depth. Lastly, we examine the use of here-and-now versus there-and-then interventions.

## TYPES OF INTERVENTIONS

To examine the types of interventions available to us as group process consultants, we will use an intervention typology matrix (see Figure 5-1).

While several intervention matrices were developed over the years, the *intervention cube* of Cohen and Smith (1976) was ground breaking. The *typology matrix* in this chapter is adapted from Cohen & Smith but modified to fit the group process consultation model.

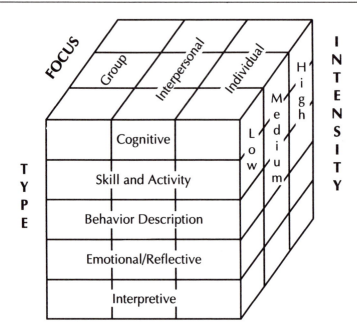

**Figure 5-1. Intervention Cube**

We categorize interventions according to *type, focus,* and *intensity.* The group process consultant chooses a combination of type, focus, and intensity each time he or she intervenes. We look first at category and then their combinations.

**Type**

There are five significant types of interventions: cognitive, skill and activity, behavior description, emotional/reflective, and interpretive.

The *cognitive* interventions are abstract, intellectual, or idea oriented. We also place consultant questions in this category. "The group might consider whether time frames are important."

The process consultant uses *skills and activities* to suggest training or some appropriate skill learning, such as a problem-solving sequence. "Let me suggest a quick practice session on giving and receiving feedback."

In the *behavior description* type, the group process consultant literally describes what he or she has observed in the group. "The group is operating as if a decision has been made, yet only two people agreed."

When the consultant reflects the emotional or feeling component observed in the group, he or she is using the fourth intervention type, *emotional/reflective*. "Fred, you seem pretty angry about Sam's remark. What's going on?"

The fifth and final type, *interpretation*, is most appropriate following a behavior description or emotional/reflective intervention. This intervention is a hypothesis or understanding of what is occurring at a dynamic level. This is conjecture on the part of the consultant. The intent is to prompt members to discuss what they think and feel about what is transpiring. It is not necessarily "truth" in an objective and analytic way. It is, however, based on the consultant's knowledge and experience. "I can only speculate that group members' lack of involvement was the reason you were sent here."

## Focus

The *focus* of the intervention may be the entire group, two or more individuals in an interpersonal interaction, or a specific individual. The following are some examples:

Group: "The level of energy in the group today is strikingly low."

Interpersonal: "Ned and Bill, I suspect your disagreement over this issue has some history to it, and the rest of us are not privy to it."

Individual: "Sally, you seem really elated whenever the group moves back to task."

## Intensity

I use *intensity* here as do Cohen and Smith (1976): the strength, power, or impact of the intervention *as the consultant intends it*. Of course, the reaction to the intervention may be different from that intended.

The intensity of an intervention can be low, medium, or high (Cohen & Smith, 1976). The consultant controls intensity primarily by choice of words, inflection of voice, and nonverbal clues such as posture. It is a prime example of using oneself as the instrument of change.

Generally, there is greater risk, higher intensity, and a greater probability of impact as the consultant moves from group to the interpersonal and on to the individual focus. Sample two interventions: "Group members seem to be irritated at the lack of progress" versus "Barney, you seem quite irritated at the lack of progress in the group." The focus of the first intervention is distributed among the members, whereas in the second, one person, Barney, is the focal point. A member may choose not to respond to the first intervention. It would be difficult for Barney not to respond to the second.

Likewise, as the consultant moves from cognitive through skill and activities, behavior description, and emotional/reflective to interpretation, there typically are greater risks, intensity, and impact. Here *risk* means uncertainty of reaction or a higher probability of intervention rejection or resistance. In the cognitive and skills-activities types, the interventions are more intellectual and can be responded to accordingly. The behavioral description is neutral; the emotional/reflective and interpretive tend to elicit more intense reactions.

The consultant's comments in the emotional/reflective and interpretive areas are inferential and subjective and require a higher level of skill. Note that the intent of these interventions is *not* psychotherapeutic. Rather, the aim of the intervention is to move the group members to explore specific dynamic levels as they relate to group effectiveness regarding the task.

The appropriateness of any intervention must relate to the life, history, and stages of group development. For example, group-focused, cognitive interventions are more appropriate and expected in the early stages of the group's life. Members are new, struggling with inclusion issues, and feeling anxious and vulnerable. To intervene with an interpretive comment—regardless of how low the intensity—is likely to be disruptive. Members at this point need a sense of psychological safety.

Emotional/reflective and interpretation interventions are more likely and appropriate as the group matures. Some groups will never warrant—or tolerate—interpretive interventions. Those groups that will must understand the nature of the interventions and contract accordingly.

## Combination Interventions

Most groups typically need some behavior description and emotional/reflective interventions to move them toward effective task accomplishment. We will now explore some of the many combinations of type, focus, and intensity.

As seen in Figure 5-2, in the group-focus, cognitive type, the group process consultant makes a simple cognitive statement

| Focus | Type | | | | |
|---|---|---|---|---|---|
| | Cognitive | Activities/Skills | Behavior Description | Emotional Reflective | Interpretive |
| **Group** | "The group seems to be behind in its completion schedule." | "Let me suggest a decision-making activity that I think you will find helpful." | "You [the group] seem to be interrupting one another in a frantic attempt to influence the outcome." | "Members are sitting on a lot of anger because you didn't influence the decision." | "The group's bitterness over past failures leads me to wonder if you are afraid to become successful." |
| **Interpersonal** | "You might both consider looking at what you have in common." | "Let me suggest that each of you write a letter to each other describing your conflict." | "The two of you are constantly supporting and protecting each other, | but when it is pointed out, you both deny it and become angry and embarrassed. | ...Is it possible that the two of you are fearful of competing with each other?" |
| **Individual** | "Tim, here is a book on the subject you might consider reading." | "Anne, why don't you take some time right now and record your thoughts and feelings in your journal." | "Whenever the group is ready to make a decision, you seem to bring up another alternative." | "It is clear that you have a great deal of affection for John but are reluctant to talk about it publicly." | "Judy, I wonder if your silence expresses anger at group members for not checking in with you?" |

**Figure 5-2. Intervention Typology Matrix**

to include the entire group. Targeting two people in the inter-personal focus, the consultant suggests a cognitive exploration. Still in the cognitive type, the consultant suggests to one individual an idea that might be helpful.

The activities-and-skills type offers structured and defined activities from which the consultant feels the group could benefit. This intervention should be used sparingly as the consultant is placed in a "training" role and one of directing the group. This role may violate the group process consultant boundary. As Figure 5-2 illustrates, the activities/skills focus suggests that the group, individuals, or a single person follow a prescribed routine, often for skill acquisition or buffered feedback. Curiously, many group process consultants never venture out of the cognitive and skills areas nor focus beyond the group. A little practice in the behavior-description type and, when appropriate, interpersonal and individual focus would greatly enhance the consultant's repertoire.

Behavior description is simply that. The group process consultant describes the behaviors he or she sees. For example, a focus on the group might generate "You seem to be interrupting one another in a frantic attempt to influence the outcome." Here the consultant describes what he or she has seen and then waits for participants to respond. We see similar descriptions with an interpersonal and individual focus.

---

### Intervention Consideration

*Use of Self.* Some group process consultants feel they should not express their own feelings or views as interventions. Consider, however, there is at least anecdotal evidence that suggests if the consultant does not first draw from the group members, they will not readily deal with conflicts. Moreover, the consultant's feelings can be offered as trial balloons as long as they are not punishing nor blaming.

Example: "I want to share with you what I am experiencing right now—and check out if it is only my perception. My energy is down and I feel as though I'm slogging through mud. Do any of you feel that way?"

When the group process consultant chooses to comment or reflect on the emotional content surrounding an event, the intervention tends to be more impactful. As always, there must be a contract in place for this type of intervention and it must be appropriate for the time and circumstances. As the examples illustrate, words are chosen to reflect the dominant feeling. Frequently, emotional/reflective interventions are used in conjunction with behavior descriptions and interpretive comments. For example, the interpersonal behavior description in Figure 5-2 is followed by an emotional/reflective comment and then an interpretation: "The two of you are constantly supporting and protecting each other," (behavior description) "but when it is pointed out, you both deny it and become angry and embarrassed" (emotional/reflective). "Is it possible that the two of you are fearful of competing with each other?" (Interpretive.)

The interpretative intervention is a speculation about what has taken place. The group process consultant offers a hypothesis or conjecture regarding the dynamics. In many groups the interpretive intervention will be neither warranted nor appropriate. However, for highly interacting groups, such as teams, in which everyone must contribute to the task solution, the interpretive intervention is both appropriate and impactful. The intent is not to psychoanalyze nor act in a therapeutic role. The intent is to ferret out what is happening in the group so that participants can move on and accomplish the task. As with all interventions, they can grow out of task or maintenance but must always be in the service of the task.

A word of caution: Emotional/reflective and interpretive interventions require a great deal of skill, particularly when they are interpersonally and personally focused. For the less experienced and beginning group process consultant, group-level interventions may be a better choice—especially in the early phases of a consultation. Moreover, it is imperative that the group process consultant has a clearly stated *contract* legitimizing these types of interventions.

The emotional/reflective and interpretive interventions are likely to be maintenance oriented and, potentially, more impactful and difficult to manage. It takes learning, skill, and practice to master all interventions but particularly emotional/reflective and interpretive. All interventions should be made with understanding, warmth, and concern.

However, group process consultation often fails because the consultant does not know how to access the dynamics of the group for all to see. The energy of the group, like it or not, lies in its socioemotional life. The truly skilled group process consultant has a complete repertoire of interventions ranging from the cognitive to the interpretive. In addition, the intensity of each type can be varied from low to high, based on *how* the consultant uses himself or herself in the expression of that intervention. It is analogous to the actor who in reading the dictionary brings the audience to tears.

## TEN CLUES THAT SOMETHING IS GOING ON

I have heard process consultants claim that they had a great repertoire of interventions and could fill out the matrix. Yet they were often unaware that anything dynamic was occurring in the group. Figure 5-3 offers *ten clues* to group dynamics. A consultant might discreetly use this brief instrument as the group works. The greater the number of items checked that deviate from the center point, 3, the greater the likelihood that *something is going on* that needs an intervention.

## 1. Goal Clarity

Do members agree on the group goal or mission? Is it clear to all? Early in the group's life, if members agree without discussing the goal, raise a red flag. As consultant, expect some initial confusion and certainly allow time to discuss the goal.

## 2. Goal Direction

The overcontrolled group and the aimless group are at bipolar points. In the former case, the members are highly structured and task oriented. Only content discussion is tolerated. Procedure is rigidly adhered to. In the latter case, there is little or no structure. Members follow any idea or procedure offered. Optimally, there needs to be a balance between structure and openness to experimentation.

**1. Goal Clarity**

| 1 | 2 | 3 | 4 | 5 |
|---|---|---|---|---|
| No Agreement | | | | Immediate Agreement |

**2. Goal Direction**

| 1 | 2 | 3 | 4 | 5 |
|---|---|---|---|---|
| Overcontrolled | | | | Aimless |

**3. Tone**

| 1 | 2 | 3 | 4 | 5 |
|---|---|---|---|---|
| Intellectual | | | | Emotional |

**4. Energy**

| 1 | 2 | 3 | 4 | 5 |
|---|---|---|---|---|
| Constricted | | Stimulating | | Frenetic |

**5. Physical Posture**

| 1 | 2 | 3 | 4 | 5 |
|---|---|---|---|---|
| Closed | | Open | | Laid Back |

**6. Tension**

| 1 | 2 | 3 | 4 | 5 |
|---|---|---|---|---|
| Brittle | | | | Effusive |

**7. Tracking**

| 1 | 2 | 3 | 4 | 5 |
|---|---|---|---|---|
| Fragmented | | | | Rigid |

**8. T/M Balance**

| 1 | 2 | 3 | 4 | 5 |
|---|---|---|---|---|
| Task Only | | Balanced | | Maintenance Only |

**9. Use of Humor**

| 1 | 2 | 3 | 4 | 5 |
|---|---|---|---|---|
| Devoid | | | | Disruptive |

**10. Use of Interventions By Group**

| 1 | 2 | 3 | 4 | 5 |
|---|---|---|---|---|
| Ignored | Rejected | Weighed | Accepted With Little Discussion | Accepted Without Discussion |

**Figure 5-3. Ten Clues to Group Dynamics**

## 3. Tone

As you listen to members interact around the task, are they intellectual and abstract or emotional? Interactive tone is characterized by the feeling behind the statements.

## 4. Energy

Although energy is somewhat difficult to define, one does see behavioral manifestations. For example, members may be verbally constricted and terse. There is little sharing or offering of ideas. Conversely, there may be a frenetic quality to the group as it works; the energy is high but seems to be "off the wall." The optimal is stimulation, that is, energy that is manageable.

## 5. Physical Posture

Closed members look that way: pulled in, arms closed, legs closed or under the chair. One would expect alertness. The other extreme is a laid back group; anything goes, totally open posture, almost a sprawling effect.

## 6. Tension

The easiest way to sense tension is around conflict. On one hand, we have a brittle group in which one feels the slightest pressure will break it apart. Members tend not to talk, particularly about what is going on. On the other hand, we have the effusive group in which verbal expression is paramount. The description might be "People were all over the place!"

## 7. Tracking

Effective groups track well both the task and the emotional well-being of the members. In less effective groups, the members do not track nor follow the task well. Ideas are not followed up. As soon as one member finishes speaking, another starts off on an entirely different topic. A member expresses some deep seated feeling; others do not respond. Instead, someone describes his or her own issue or concern. The process is patently fragmented.

Conversely, in other groups, the tracking is so rigid there is no room for any deviation. This is particularly true in content- and task-oriented groups. The task process is slavishly followed. Stopping to check on members' needs becomes a major disruption in itself.

## 8. Task/ Maintenance Balance

As discussed in other chapters, there needs to be an optimal balance between task process and maintenance process. Too much task focus, and the energy and emotional needs of the group members suffer. Likewise, an overfocused maintenance process can lead to an ineffective group that does not complete the task.

### 9. Use of Humor

Groups that are devoid of humor are deadly, dull, stultifying, and generally unproductive. However, too much humor is disruptive. Initially it may be "fun" and offer comic relief. It soon becomes unsatisfying for the members and equally unproductive. Humor is desirable, offers relief from tension, and helps members bond; balance is required, however.

### 10. Use of Interventions by Group

When the group process consultant intervenes, he or she can expect a range of reactions. Consistently ignoring or rejecting interventions by the group denies dynamics that need exploring. Indeed, the dynamics may have something to do with the relationship between group members and the consultant. When the group consistently accepts the consultant's interventions with little or no discussion, it is also time to be suspicious. Weighing interventions, then appropriately rejecting or accepting them is the expectation. Behavioral extremes without weighing indicates hidden group issues.

---

### Intervention Consideration

*Ten Clues.* Use any one of the "Ten Clues" as an intervention, particularly in behavioral description.

Example: "Let me check this out with you. Is it my distortion or is this group deadly serious? I haven't heard any attempts at humor in an hour. What's going on?"

---

As stated earlier, one clue may not be enough to raise the consultant's awareness. However, clues operating simultaneously invariably indicate covert dynamics. The group process consultant looks for the nature of the dynamics and decides how and how deep to intervene. We now turn to determining the depth of the intervention.

In many ways the task group is like the H.M.S. Titanic steaming toward the iceberg. Consider the group members as passengers on a ship; those managers, consultants, and leaders responsible for effective maintenance and task accomplishment are the crew. On a ship there may be a general objective—a distant port—but no nautical map to show how to get there. Moreover, the crew may be unskilled and without contingency plans in case of trouble; the passengers have their own, usually implicit, agendas. There is a fantasy held by the captain that the ship is unsinkable.

Work groups, too, can be headed for disaster. There is a distant objective but no solid plan for arriving there. Group members are unskilled and unaware of the skills required for effective task completion. Contingency plans are not formulated or even considered. Members have their own styles, ideas, and agenda. The manager has his or her own ideas on how to reach the objective and may not consider any others. This could be a dysfunctional group without the manager's knowledge.

In any group setting there exists an "iceberg" of dynamics. There is the stated work to be done, the *content*, that is above the water line (see Figure 5-4). It is overt and usually agreed on by members. Below the surface, however, are the hidden or covert task and maintenance dynamics. *These dynamics generate the energy for what evolves behaviorally and determine how effectively the group will move toward its stated objectives.* It is on these task and maintenance dynamics that the group process consultant intervenes. Group dynamics are *very* complex and exist simultaneously at multiple levels—some overt, others covert.

Figure 5-4 illustrates five levels at which any given dynamics exist and where the consultant can choose to intervene. Level I is primarily content, above the surface and easily observable. The group process consultant does not intervene around content.

In Level II are those behaviors that are primarily overt. They are right at the surface, observable to the discerning eye. Sometimes Level II behaviors are covert, just below the surface.

Levels III and IV must be inferred from the behavior patterns seen in Levels I and II. Level V, the unconscious, is, by definition, inaccessible. Theoretically, it is the *probable origin*

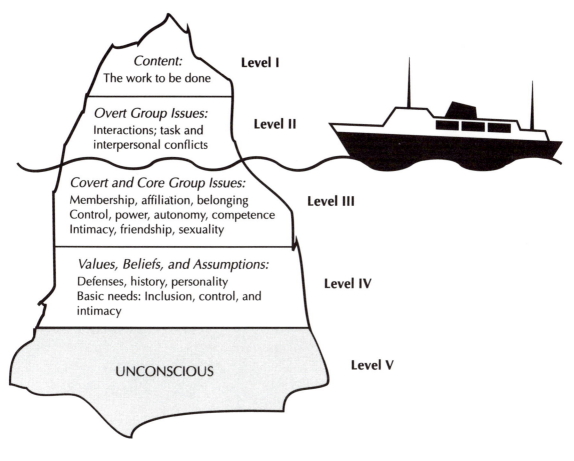

*Content:*
The work to be done     **Level I**

*Overt Group Issues:*
Interactions; task and
interpersonal conflicts     **Level II**

*Covert and Core Group Issues:*
Membership, affiliation, belonging    **Level III**
Control, power, autonomy, competence
Intimacy, friendship, sexuality

*Values, Beliefs, and Assumptions:*
Defenses, history, personality     **Level IV**
Basic needs: Inclusion, control, and
intimacy

UNCONSCIOUS     **Level V**

**Figure 5-4. Iceberg of Group Dynamics**

of the dynamics that eventually emerge in Levels I through IV. The unconscious is the reservoir of one's basic instincts, motivations, impulses, and unacceptable wishes. It is not readily accessible to normal awareness, nor is it is appropriate for the group process consultant to focus attention in this area. To do so could be disruptive to the group and potentially destructive to a group member. Unconscious dynamics may be explored appropriately only within the professional boundaries of some individual and group psychotherapies.

The preceding level influences the dynamics of each following level. It is within this context that the effective group process consultant chooses what *depth* to make an intervention and in what *form*. If the group process consultant knows how to intervene at only one level, he or she is courting task failure and member dissatisfaction. Let us examine each level in detail.

## Level I

Focal in Level I is content only—the work, task, project, or service. *How* group members accomplish the task and how they *feel* about what they are doing or interacting are not considered here. Considered in Level I is only the *what*.

## Level II

In Level II we consider the basic and obvious member interactions and task behaviors. They are observable at the surface or just below the surface. Group members or the consultant may not refer to them explicitly. How group members present themselves, deal with conflict, solve problems, and make decisions are seen here. Who talks to whom and under what circumstances? Do members follow through on task? Do some fail to see the urgency? What does it take to become a member of this group? What are the obvious norms around inclusion, control, and affection? (Schutz, 1958)

## Level III

It is at Level III that we infer the *core group issues*. It is a covert level and, of course, gives rise to the behaviors and dynamics we observed in Level II. Working with these dynamics is often critical to the success of the group. The group process consultant working at this level is *accessing the core*.

The major dynamics here are what we *infer* from the Level II behaviors. They are typically issues of inclusion, belonging, control and power, independence, competence, autonomy, intimacy, and sexuality. The "isms" are found in Level III: racism, sexism, and ageism.

There are only a few *core* generic issues that give rise to the complex dynamics we experience in the group setting. The complexity has to do with multilevels. Think for a moment of any behavioral example, current or past, you have observed in a group setting. The chances are such that dynamically your example will fit into one of a few general categories as described above. The work of Schutz (1958) supports this contention.

Schutz proposed that people have three basic interpersonal needs that are shown in behavior and feelings toward others. These behaviors and feelings grow out of one's self-concept. The basic need areas are *inclusion, control,* and *affection.*

Inclusion refers to feelings about being important or significant, of having some worth so that people will care. The aspect of the self-concept related to control is the feeling of competence, including intelligence, appearance, practicality, and a general ability to cope with the world. The area of affection revolves around feelings of being lovable and feeling that if one's personal core is revealed in its entirety it will be seen as a lovely thing (Schutz, 1971).

*Inclusion*

We see the dynamics of inclusion as group members struggle for membership and finding a place in the group where they can contribute: "How can I be prominent and have an identity in this group?"

In inclusion behaviors we experience the caution and tight conformity of group members. Some members are reluctant to enter into any interactions. Others plunge into interactions. Some members pair or coalesce with others who have similar backgrounds or who have similar attitudes around the task.

*Control*

Control dynamics are manifest around decision making and issues of competence, power, authority, and influence. Following instructions, compliance, and submission all relate to the control dynamic.

Schutz (1967, p. 19) describes control as "the effort to achieve enough influence so that a man can determine his future to the degree that he finds most comfortable, and to relinquish enough control so that he is able to lean on others to teach, guide, support, and at times to take some responsibility from him."

Who is going to lead this group? The group process consultant will observe the shifting sands of power as different group members vie for influence. Group members may turn toward—or upon—the consultant for direction and venting hostility. Dependent members struggle with counterdependent members and a schism is created.

## Affection

Schutz (1958, p. 20) behaviorally defines affection as "the need to establish and maintain a satisfactory relation with others with respect to love and affection."

Affection dynamics are played out in how near or far toward people we will permit ourselves. Will I be accepted in this group as a person of value? If I go against the group, will I no longer be liked? What is the price of cohesion in this group? Will it necessitate a degree of intimacy through disclosure?

As the group becomes cohesive and close, is there generated an overoptimism about the product? As the group moves toward its goals, some members may withdraw because of the anticipated separation.

Within Level III, lies the critical energy of any group. Because dynamics may not be dealt with *at this level,* the group becomes bogged down, arrested, or immobilized. The end result: Members are dissatisfied; work is not accomplished; absenteeism increases; creativity is stultified.

Lawrence LeShan (1974) relates two folk tales that speak to the dynamics of Level III. The first, an old Sufi analogy, involves the example of a chariot. A person who knows direction is required to actively drive the chariot. The state of emotion is represented by the horse (the true force) that pulls the chariot. The intellect is the chariot itself. As LeShan points out, all three are necessary, but the driver must be in command.

In our context, the group process consultant is the driver, and the content is represented by the chariot. The emotion and energy of the group is the power of the horse. It pulls in many directions with intensity. To ignore the energy and focus only on the chariot or content is to court disaster.

A second story repeated by LeShan is a Hasidic tale. He describes the criticism of a type of Habad Hasidism that focused primarily on the will and intellect, neglecting emotional life: "...it was like turning out a good marksman who knew how to aim and fire his rifle and knew the target. The only problem was that there was no powder in his bullets" (p. 44). Again, in our context the powder is the emotional life of the group. This must be tapped for growth and productivity. The group process consultant may know how to make interventions and may have the sense of direction. However, if he or she cannot focus on the emotional aspects of the group, like the Hasidic criticism, he or she will not be successful.

Intervention at Level III may not be appropriate for all groups nor done with high frequency in others. Still, the group process consultant must be particularly sensitive to dynamics at this level. Moreover, he or she must be capable of intervening at this level in order to move some groups forward. Caution must be given to interventions at Level III. The consultant may inadvertently intervene at this level when the group is not ready. Fortunately, when this happens, group members typically ignore the consultant or think his or her intervention is "off the wall."

## Level IV

At Level IV, we focus on the values, beliefs, and assumptions we hold about the world. These include defense mechanisms, history, and personality. Our very basic *interpersonal needs* ascend here: belonging, identity, mastery over the environment, and intimacy. These are the *least* changeable characteristics of the individual.

In most organizational settings, although there are exceptions, we do not target these dynamics. They are, however, the subject and focus in personal growth groups and sensitivity training. Like other levels, the dynamics in Level IV give rise to those of Level III. Exploration of Level IV dynamics are typically not appropriate in the organizational and work setting. This is probably one of the reasons that during the 1960s sensitivity training developed a poor image and bad reputation within corporate America. Practitioners were readily exploring the dynamics of Level IV. Group members found this highly disclosing, confronting, too personal, and disruptive.

## Level V

Since Level V is unconscious, one assumes that the dynamics are deeply hidden. They are inaccessible to the individual and to the process consultant. Working with unconscious material is certainly not within the purview of the group process consultant. It must be left to group psychotherapy or individual reconstructive therapies.

The following two examples show the choices the consultant has in any situation.

### Scenario I

The group has convened to discuss a new assignment. Jerry reminds members what happened the last time they worked together and suggests a new start, building on what they have learned. This starts an outpouring of humorous and then negative remembrances. Members' comments become vague and indirectly accusatory as they recount their failed past projects.

At Level II, the group process consultant might use a *behavior description* and intervene: "Jerry suggested a new start, but it's been ignored in favor of reliving your past failures." Here we see a simple description without inferences. It merely captures what is happening at the moment, the observable overt behavior, but may lead the group to generate their own, higher level interpretation.

The group process consultant at Level III might intervene with an *emotional/reflective* comment: "The group seems intent on assigning blame for incidents that are long past. Any ideas why you are so angry with one another?" In this intervention, the process consultant initiates a deeper exploration. Not only does he or she reflect the emotional content, the consultant also asks what is behind the anger.

An *interpretive* intervention at Level IV might be: "Your anger over past failures seems to be getting in the way of your working together. Perhaps each of you is fearful of success..." The choice of the consultant here is to offer a hypothesis on what might be going on and suggest that individuals examine their own behavior. Although the consultant has some notion about the dynamics involved, the speculative intervention does not have to be "truth." The idea is to get members to talk about what is going on and, at this level, to examine themselves.

As you can see, each intervention taps into a deeper level. While the sequence of behavior-description, emotional/reflective, and interpretive interventions do not have to be used in conjunction with the specific levels, these interventions do lend themselves quite nicely.

## Scenario II

The group is discussing personal-best experiences as a team member. All group members have mentioned or have been asked about their personal and professional experiences except Sally.

At Level II, overt behavior, a behavior description might be used: "No one has asked Sally about her experiences." The intervention is made. The consultant waits for members to respond accordingly.

In Level III, the consultant chooses to intervene a bit deeper and explore the issue of Sally's inclusion: "Sally, given that you haven't been asked by others about your experiences, where are you with the group at this time? And where are the rest of you with Sally?"

Finally, in a Level IV intervention, the group process consultant speculates about Sally's anger: "Sally, does your silence indicate anger at group members for not checking in with you?"

It must be restated that a range and mixture of focus, type, and intensity will elicit the depth wanted by the group process consultant. However, as always, the intervention is made in the service of the task. Roger Harrison (1970) admonishes consultants "to intervene at a level no deeper than that required to produce enduring solutions to the problems at hand" (p. 190) and "to intervene at a level no deeper than that at which the energy and resources of the client can be committed to problem solving and to change" (p. 198). Although Harrison was speaking of organization consultants in general, his words are especially apropos to group process consultation. A further examination of the dimensions will help the group process consultant know what level to choose and when.

## CHOOSING THE DEPTH OF INTERVENTION

How does the group process consultant know how deep to intervene at any given time? What must he or she weigh? Let us look at eight dimensions associated with the readiness of a group to use differing depths of intervention: (1) initial contract; (2) type of group; (3) nature of the task; (4) content versus process orientation; (5) frequency and duration of meetings; (6) expected life of the group; (7) stage of group development; and (8) psychological mindedness.

### Initial Contract

A major boundary determinant of where to intervene is the final version of the initial contract. The client needs to know the consultant's expectations and intervention style. If the consultant believes that the type of group and the nature of the task warrant intense interventions, he or she must convey this to the group members. He or she gives examples so that members understand exactly what will happen—and the potential risks involved. The members must then "buy in" to the contract to make it happen. Over 75 percent of failed consultations could probably be traced to no contract or an inadequate contract. Rarely do consultants articulate descriptions of their interventions. Thus, when a consultant makes an emotional/reflective intervention, group members are unprepared, if not mystified or shocked. When there is a clear understanding of the contract by both the client and the consultant, there are rarely any surprises.

### Type of Group

The type of group with which the consultant is working will help determine the depth of intervention. It is unlikely that the group process consultant will make a Level IV intervention in an ad hoc group that is meeting for a short time. This is particularly true regarding a moderately simple problem. Conversely, it is both appropriate and necessary if a research-and-development group works on a complex set of tasks over an extended period and the profitability of the company rides on the outcome. The group process consultant will intervene at deeper levels in order to tap the energy and creativity of the group. Again, this is made explicit in the contract following the completion of a "readiness assessment."

## Nature of the Task

If the nature of the group task is clear and technical and requires information rather than interaction, interventions should be made at levels near the surface rather than those of deeper levels. When the nature of the task is ambiguous and relies on the pooled resources of all group members, the consequent inter-actions and generated dynamics will necessitate more depth-oriented interventions.

## Content Versus Process Orientation

Regardless of the nature of their tasks, many groups are simply content oriented. The reasons are varied. It is part style, part training, part organization. Openness may not be a norm in the organization; conflict may be an anathema, and interpersonal feedback may be verboten. In other settings and cultures, there is greater openness. The norms allow group members to readily interact and deal directly with conflict, recognizing its creative potential.

If, in the initial assessment, the group process consultant determines that the group is highly content oriented or has little tolerance for process, be it task or maintenance, it is most effective to intervene primarily at Level II. Chapter Three discussed the use of the "Team Orientation and Behavior Inventory" (Goodstein, Cooke, & Goodstein, 1983) as a means to determine process value and skills. The results will give both consultant and group members a diagnostic look regarding where they perceive themselves on these dimensions.

## Frequency and Duration of Meetings

When group meetings are infrequent and of short duration, that is, less than an hour and a half, intervening at any of the deeper levels is counterindicated. The group simply does not have enough time to become cohesive or to gel. Quality circles and quality teams offer a good example. One reason so many quality circles fail is simply because groups are not permitted enough time to meet. Moreover, many circles do not meet frequently or regularly. *Members are individuals in a group setting,* versus a group. They are not work cohesive to accomplish a set of complex tasks. A simple but powerful intervention is to suggest to the group or team that they meet more frequently and for longer periods.

## Expected Life of the Group

Groups that expect to complete their work in a short time will typically resist depth-oriented interventions. However, if group members are sophisticated and experienced in maintenance interventions—and they contract with the consultant for such— then the process consultant can intervene in Level III for greater impact. This will speed the group to more efficiently and effectively complete the task. Again, this happens only when group members have worked together previously or have participated in groups that were maintenance oriented.

In groups that prevail for an extended period, the process consultant has a wider range of intervention options. All groups, whether of long- or short-life expectancy, should establish time boundaries. Groups will operate more effectively if they know when they expect to terminate.

## Stage of Group Development

Regardless of the theory of group development the consultant chooses, the stage will influence the depth of intervention. New groups in their early stage are probably not responsive to depth-oriented interventions. Instead, the consultant needs to spend his or her time creating a safe climate in which the group can work. The consultant must model honest but not overly intense behavior.

## Psychological Mindedness

Simply, many group members are not psychologically minded. They strongly resist the notions of maintenance, feelings, and individual focus. This is particularly true in many corporate settings. They are conflict avoidant. Norms do not allow major issues to be dealt with within the group; these issues are taken "off line." However, when major issues are taken out of the group, trust is not developed. Group members cannot learn how to deal with one another, share issues, and create. In general, effective work and group productivity is thwarted.

## DEPTH AND TYPE OF GROUP

Figure 5-5 permits us to examine the implications of using the "Iceberg of Group Dynamics." The first two columns list the levels and major focus of each. Column three indicates the depth of intervention from low to high. The greater the depth, the greater the emotional risk for the group or individuals focused on. "Risk" here means the unpredictability of reaction. Of course, one also expects a greater intensity and, potentially, a greater impact on the group—assuming the intervention is appropriate.

Column four illustrates *group life*, with the cognitive (abstract ideas, questions, procedures, etc.) located primarily in Levels I and II. The emotional component, which accounts for the intensity of group life, resides in Levels II through V.

Column five gives the process mix. As the consultant focuses on the emotional aspects of the group, he or she will probably make fewer task interventions and more maintenance interventions. When the group process consultant chooses to move in this direction, the intervention changes accordingly, and appropriately, from the group focus to the interpersonal and personal foci. Again, there is wide overlap. The consultant can be expected to focus interventions *in any group setting* on the group as a whole, the interpersonal combinations, and the individual. However, the frequency of group-focused interventions will be higher when operating in Levels II versus a higher frequency of the interpersonal and personal interventions when operating in Levels III through IV.

From column six, group examples, we can infer some rules of thumb for the demands of various group types. For example, if a group convenes only to share information, it is likely that the target of the group process consultant's interventions will be strictly the task. It is unlikely, and probably inappropriate, for the consultant to intervene at a deeper level. The work of quality circles necessitates that some interventions go beyond the task and move into the maintenance area. Many teams, groups, and

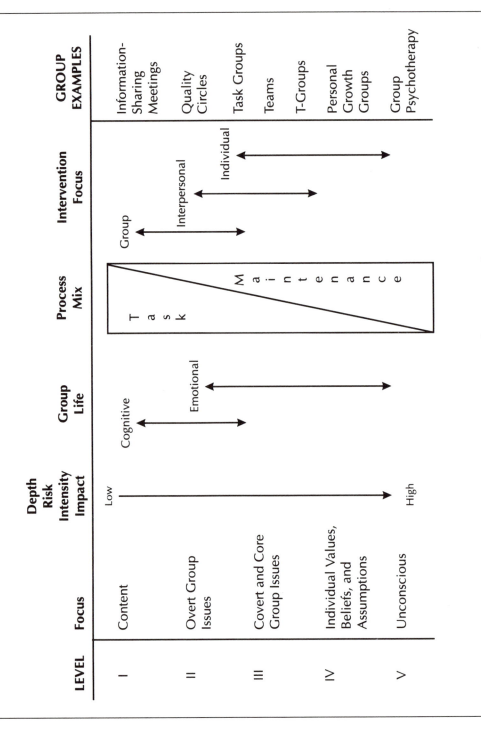

**Figure 5-5. Intervention Dynamics**

The figure is organized as a table with the following columns: LEVEL, Focus, Depth Risk Intensity Impact, Group Life, Process Mix, Intervention Focus, and GROUP EXAMPLES.

| LEVEL | Focus | Depth Risk Intensity Impact | Group Life | Process Mix | Intervention Focus | GROUP EXAMPLES |
|---|---|---|---|---|---|---|
| I | Content | Low | Cognitive | Task / Maintenance | Group | Information-Sharing Meetings |
| II | Overt Group Issues | | Emotional | | Interpersonal | Quality Circles |
| III | Covert and Core Group Issues | | | | | Task Groups |
| IV | Individual Values, Beliefs, and Assumptions | | | | Individual | Teams |
| | | | | | | T-Groups |
| | | | | | | Personal Growth Groups |
| V | Unconscious | High | | | | Group Psychotherapy |

circles fail partly because the consultants, leaders, and facilitators are trained only in structured interventions. They do not have the knowledge nor the skills in the socioemotional aspects of the group. We know the primary *energy* of the group lies at a deeper level. Periodically, the group process consultant must explore the maintenance dynamics of the group.

This is also the case for task groups, particularly those that meet over an extended period. Teams, because of their required high interactive nature, must of necessity use both task and maintenance interventions. They help members reach their objectives and permit member satisfaction. It is necessary and appropriate to *access the core* (Level III) when facilitating team building. Indeed, if there is a consultant-team contract for both task and maintenance interventions, and if the intervention is warranted, the group process consultant may at times target interventions in Level IV.

While few T-groups and personal growth groups are currently conducted in-house, at least in their pure form, they are offered publicly. Strangers constitute the membership. In these groups, it is both desirable and appropriate to explore personal and interpersonal issues, individual values, beliefs, and assumptions. This requires of the consultant competence in Level IV interventions.

---

### Intervention Consideration

*Metaphors* serve as powerful interventions. Develop a core list for your "kit bag." However, group members must relate to them.

Examples: Sports, garden, nature, and machines.

Metaphors cannot be esoteric or they will, in consultation parlance, "bomb." Comparing the group to Queen Anne furniture may not be helpful.

Examples:

1. "At times the group is running toward the goal line—but in the wrong direction."
2. "If this group were a garden, how would you describe your work?"

---

## DEPTH AND INTERVENTION SELECTION

We now turn to selecting *types* of interventions from the typology matrix in order to optimize *depth* of intervention. For example, intervening in Level II is accomplished by a behavior description. The consultant simply describes what he or she has observed. Accessing the core in Level III usually requires an emotional/reflective intervention, often following a behavior description. If the contract and stage permit, an interpretive intervention may also be appropriate. Level IV more often requires an interpretive intervention. While these are general guidelines, there are many exceptions. Much depends on the skill of the group process consultant and his or her ability to use himself or herself as the agent of change. Some consultants appropriately use a low intensity interpretive intervention to get at dynamics in Level II. However, this takes considerable skill and experience.

## HERE AND NOW VERSUS THERE AND THEN

The most powerful interventions are made in the *here and now*. The process consultant focuses on what is happening in the group *at the moment it occurs*. For example, Fred attempts to give Art feedback regarding Art's consistent interruptions. Art interrupts Fred to defend his behavior. The consultant uses this immediate situation to point out to Art that the way he is behaving *at the moment* is exactly the behavior about which Fred is giving him feedback. If this were a *there-and-then* intervention, the consultant would wait until a later time to refocus on Art's behavior. The *there and then* refers back to a prior point in time.

The power of the here-and-now intervention is that it is *in the immediate experience* of the target person's awareness as well as in the group members' experience. As a consultant-modeling strategy, it is very powerful. Even the most defensive person is impacted by the here-and-now intervention. Of course, the group process consultant must be alert to the occurrence of here-and-now incidents and phrase them in such a way that group members will not be embarrassed at being caught. Incidents are easy to miss. Intervention phraseology must convey support and concern and be in the focal person's best interest.

A second common example occurs when group members are discussing, in the abstract, a situation or set of behaviors. They are oblivious to the possibility that the same dynamics operate in their own group. For example, members discuss other groups in which people are "always interrupting one another." The process consultant intervenes, "Could that same behavior, the interruptions, be happening in here?"

One can assume *whatever the group talks about relates to the dynamics of the present group.* While this concept emanated in group psychotherapy, it is relevant to other groups, teams, and committees. "We assume that the content of the session, no matter how seemingly remote, refers to here-and-now relationships and feelings in the group" (Whitaker & Lieberman, 1964, p. 17).

## Metaphors

A special case of powerful here-and-now interventions derives from the use of metaphors. Group members fell into a discussion of "jigsaw puzzles." Two members stated that they had difficulty in putting puzzles together; they found this frustrating and annoying. The group process consultant asked if the group could see any parallels between what the group was discussing and behaviors in the present group. This led to an intense discussion among members regarding their anger about what was happening in their group and their inability to understand the dynamics. *They could not put the pieces together.*

Other common examples relate to sports and games (e.g., football or golf). The group process consultant might ask, "What games are being played in this group?" Explosions, firecrackers, burning, etc., also appear frequently: "Perhaps something is about to explode here" or "What blow-ups are we preventing?"

Is the then-and-there intervention ever appropriate? Absolutely. It is particularly useful when the consultant wishes to refrain from intervening until he or she has more data. The consultant may wish to see if the group will raise or resolve an issue on its own. The consultant may also wish to hold off to determine if the behaviors will form a more consistent pattern. When the time is opportune, the consultant shares with the group members what he or she has been observing. However, after the there-and-then intervention, the consultant needs to make here-and-now interventions about the behaviors he or she has described.

Chapter Six traces stages of work group activity from the consultant's vantage point. Under each stage, task and maintenance dimensions are detailed.

## Executive Planning Team ◆ ◆ ◆

During the next meeting the team finally agreed on their charge and how to systematically approach it. Team members' strong personalities and aggressiveness often resulted in confrontations, not listening, and members' putting their needs ahead of the organization. Scott intervened frequently, helping keep members on track and giving them the opportunity to express feelings about the work, one another, and their progress.

Although these managers had insisted that their subordinates learn a problem-solving sequence, only one manager had bothered to do so. Scott suggested Bill teach the others the approach. (Intervention: skills and activities type; personal focus; low intensity; task oriented.) Members strongly supported this suggestion. Bill was obviously pleased. The next meeting he came equipped with transparencies and workbook materials. He used one of the team's identified problems as an example. The session was very successful and served to bring the group closer together.

## Quality Circles ◆ ◆ ◆

*Circle I.* During a session when she thought in-group competition was again close to the surface, Kim drew a simple picture on the flip chart. It was a carpet and a broom. She asked, "What are the issues and concerns in this group that, at the moment, are being swept under the rug? I mean things you aren't talking about that may be inhibiting the group's effectiveness. When you feel you are ready, go up to the chart, and write down the issues with a marker." (Intervention: skills and activities type; group focus; low intensity; maintenance oriented.)

There was some laughter among the group. After a minute or so, Zeb arose and wrote, "Uneven contribution." Phil added, "Leadership" and "Competition." Landau wrote, "Product ownership." Others were added: "Nobody listening," "Too little time," and "Big egos."

Zeb's comment brought an uneasy laughter: "There's a lot of stuff we aren't dealing with."

Kim suggested they each use two straw votes to prioritize the issues they should start to deal with. Each member went to the flip chart and checked off their priorities. *Competition* was the clear winner, followed by *ownership*. *Uneven contribution* was third.

As the session ended, Kim suggested members give some thought to the results and decide how they wanted to deal with the issues.

*Circle II*. Michael became more comfortable at risking new interventions. His behavioral descriptions were clearer and more precise. He ventured more into the interpersonal areas, both overt and covert. However, when a member would directly challenge Michael, he continued to become flustered and sometimes defensive. He knew he "took things too personally."

A critical incident occurred during a session late one afternoon. Shelly and Chip had a confrontation and Michael intervened. Shelly turned and challenged Michael's perception and intervention. Michael stammered, defended his intervention, and tried to move on. The group, however, would not let him escape. Shelly challenged, "Why is it you expect us to deal with conflict but back off when it comes to you?"

Michael reluctantly admitted he was made anxious by conflict. Moreover, he feared that his interventions, few as they were, would fuel rather than help the conflict. (Intervention: consultant self-disclosure.)

"You mean you have as much a problem as we do?" Chip asked incredulously.

"Yes, I'm afraid I do."

"Boy, do I feel better hearing that! It makes you seem like one of us. By the way, I think your comments to us—to me anyway—are really helpful." There was much head nodding and several yeses.

Then someone added, "Yes, I think you should continue what you've been doing around the conflict, too."

Michael felt an enormous sense of relief—and empowerment. He also wished he had talked about his feelings earlier but knew he had been afraid. He now felt more committed to the group than ever and also to the process.

*Circle III.* Larry did not mention again the question of adding new members to Circle III. His quality circle continued for another two months but attendance dropped off; members arrived late or left early. At one point Larry intervened: "Does anyone mind that attendance is off?" (Intervention: cognitive type; group focus; low intensity; maintenance oriented.)

Les was the only member to comment: "Not really."

A couple of members laughed; the rest remained silent. It was not discussed further.

Larry made an appointment with the team sponsor, the human resource manager, who was instructed to create the quality teams.

## Hospital Administration ♦ ♦ ♦

At the next meeting, surprisingly, Ned suggested, "Let's put those norms together."

The group readily agreed, probably thinking the norms might help keep Ned in check. In twenty minutes the group developed the following:

- Start meetings on time.
- Don't interrupt.
- Paraphrase when asked.
- Confront ideas; support people.
- Everyone contribute—but less than a minute at a time.

- Check every thirty minutes on how we are doing.
- End meetings on time.

Laura suggested they make two copies on poster board and post them on both sides of the work room. (Intervention: cognitive type; group focus; low intensity; task oriented.) This was agreed on and done by the next meeting.

# Phases of Task-Group Development

# 6

*W*hat the field does not need is another treatise on group development. However, most current theories have been developed from the vantage point and experience of the participant (Tuckman, 1965; Schutz, 1958; Bennis & Shepard, 1948). What I propose here instead is an analysis of the phases of *work-group activity* from the perspective of the group process consultant; that is, what the phases are through which the work group evolves and are influenced by the consultant's interventions.

## THE FOUR PHASES

Various behaviors and issues must be attended to in each phase, so the group proceeds effectively toward attaining both its task completion and member satisfaction. Figure 6-1 illustrates four phases and the expected frequency with which the consultant makes task and maintenance interventions.

This chapter presents a brief overview of the four phases and then examines each phase in detail.

In the *setting-up* phase, members are new to the group, although they may know each other. They are also new to the project or charge. It is expected that members may be a bit apprehensive about roles, membership, and charge to the group.

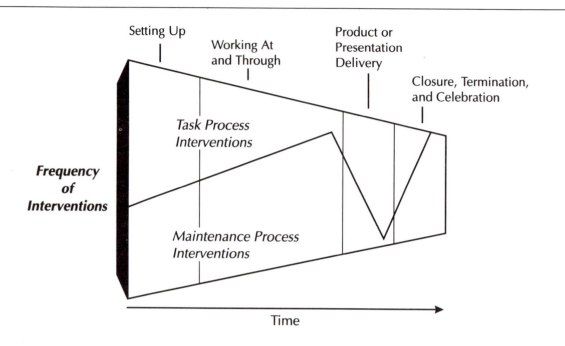

**Figure 6-1. Consultant Stages of Work Group Activity**

If they are skilled and experienced, they will set an agenda and clarify their task.

Quite likely, members will not know how to proceed or will be reluctant to offer suggestions to the group. The group process consultant will need to intervene frequently, focusing on both these task and maintenance concerns. Although all the phases vary in length, depending on the group, setting up takes no more than six two-hour meetings and perhaps as few as three meetings. Moreover, the phase boundary in setting up is typically well marked. That is, the group process consultant knows clearly when the group has moved into the *working-at-and-through* phase. When groups avoid or short circuit the setting up, they become bogged down and stuck. Members become irritated, withdraw, or want to push ahead at all costs. This is common in groups that do not set agendas, plan, nor agree on next steps and procedures.

The *working-at-and-through* phase occupies the greatest amount of time for the consultant and group members. Indeed, there is much we do not know about the middle phases of work groups, nor how to intervene. It is more art than science. Group process consultants describe their "stuck points" as occurring most frequently during the working-at-and-through phase. As the name of this phase implies, the team or group is working *at* task and working *through* maintenance. Overt and covert issues around task completion and group member satisfaction emerge during this phase. The group process consultant must attend to them and help manage the process accordingly. As the group moves through this phase there is an increase in maintenance focus—as it relates to task—and a decrease in task focus. This does not mean that there is no task activity. It does mean that as the group works on complex, and often ambiguous, problems, it requires high interaction and thus a greater degree of maintenance.

As the deadline for product or presentation delivery approaches, many subtasks are required. (This is appropriately called the *product-or-presentation-delivery* phase.) The group process consultant offers suggestions on how to deal with the details. Maintenance issues, if not yet resolved, may be put aside in preparation for delivery. If they are not, they must be worked by the group with the help of the consultant, so that delivery is properly executed. This phase is usually quite short in length and, if the group has worked through its issues, one of anticipation and excitement.

When the presentation is over or the product is delivered, there is a final phase of *closure, termination, and* (ideally) *celebration.* Unfortunately, groups, teams, and staffs do not typically celebrate their accomplishments and successes.

Groups also often terminate without managing closure. In fact, not managing closure and not celebrating accomplishments may be such an established norm that the group process consultant has to work hard to get the group to examine issues growing out of task completion. Do group members feel satisfied with what they accomplished? How do they feel about one another? How do they feel about separating after much time spent together? What have group members learned that they can now transfer to new situations? What pitfalls could now be avoided? Has the group been celebrating milestones throughout it phases? How can the group now celebrate its final accomplishments? Possibilities include verbally, with affirmations from all; a memento; a write-up in the organization newsletter; or a ball game or party together, with or without friends or spouses.

This final phase, like the preceding phase, is usually short in duration, but it is important that the group move through this phase and examine the issues found here.

Optimally, as the consultant works through the four phases, he or she uses fewer interventions. The incidence of task interventions are typically higher in the first phases of the group's life. Maintenance interventions increase as task interventions decrease. However, there is a spike in task interventions as the group approaches delivery time for their product, report, or presentation. The final stage, with the exception of some follow-up tasks, is primarily maintenance focused, although the frequency of interventions tend to be considerably lower than in the initial phase.

We will now examine each phase in detail from several perspectives: general observable behavior, task issues, maintenance issues, group process consultant behaviors, and group process consultant interventions.

## SETTING UP

### General Description

The initial group, staff, or team meeting is fascinating and sometimes humorous to observe, primarily because it is so predictable (Figure 6-2). Even when group members know one another, the start-up is similar. There is the usual stiff acquaintance: "Do you know so and so?" Members may posture, "I've been in a lot of these groups and here's what we can expect." Members are overpolite and for the most part show low assertiveness. A couple of members, in an attempt to manage anxiety, may be abrupt and even aggressive. Status in this early phase is usually based on position and role outside the group.

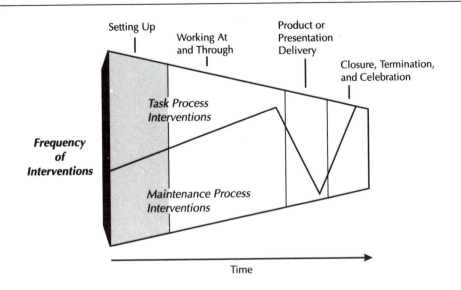

Figure 6-2. Setting Up

Comments often seem random and very little listening takes place. An idea may be tentatively offered. No one responds. The next comment is totally unrelated. Task and maintenance skills, if held, are not in evidence. Group members look to the designated leader for structure and direction. If direction is not forthcoming, members still resist taking on the responsibility and ownership for group success.

The dynamics of Schutz' (1958) *inclusion* stage are seen during setting up as are Tuckman's (1965) *forming* and Bennis and Shepard's (1948) subphase, *dependence-submission.*

**Task**

In most work groups, the initial and *overt* concerns will be around task. Even with an explicit charge, ambiguity prevails. The group process consultant must first deal with these concerns to make members comfortable and empowered to work on the task.

Concretely, the group process consultant will need to be aware of and focus on the following task concerns:

- Goal clarity
- Formal roles:
    Time keeper

    Scribe

    Leader

    Facilitator
- Available task resources
- Task-skill competence
- Idea tracking

---

### Intervention Consideration

*Tyranny of the Flip Chart.* How often have you been in an initial group meeting and, when the charge or task is given, someone jumps up to the flip chart and starts writing or brainstorming? Too many groups are solution oriented rather than problem oriented. Moreover, as soon as someone is at the flip chart, the group configuration becomes a horseshoe, instead of a circle, and members talk to the chart or scribe rather than to one another.

Arrive at the meeting a bit early and close down the easels. Before anyone begins to scribe, suggest the group spend some time talking about how they feel about being in the group and working on this particular task. A problem orientation can be suggested and procedures defined before any writing is done.

---

## Maintenance

The initial maintenance issues are typically covert or at least not disclosed publicly. Members do not want to appear or be different at this phase. The issues and concerns, of course, are there, but under wraps. "Do I belong here? Will I fit in? Will people like me? How will the group members act toward me? I don't have a good feeling about...!"

Members are cautious. They test out one another in subtle ways. Openness is not likely to be a norm. Members keep feelings hidden. They are reluctant to appear different or to exhibit vulnerabilities. Conformity at this point seems to be a group membership requirement. Specifically, we are looking at issues around the following:

- Inclusion
- Membership
- Belonging
- Dependency
- Risk of openness and disclosure
- Comfort:
    Physical
    Psychological
- Working climate
- Involvement
- Contributions
- Identity with group

**Consultant Behaviors**

The consultant works the maintenance-process and task-process issues. Although task-process issues will be paramount, the consultant must first establish rapport, visibility, credibility, and psychological safety. An immediate, clear contract will help a great deal. Warmth, humor, attention, listening, paraphrasing, physically leaning in, nondefensiveness, suggestions, and recommendations are important.

Consider the following example:

An internal group process consultant was assigned to a cross-functional work team. The organization was in crisis; all employees—particularly the managers—were feeling the stress of overwork. Team members had also been *assigned*. There was much grumbling when the members sat down for the first group meeting.

"Let's get on with this s——," muttered one obviously unhappy manager.

"Sounds like you'd rather be doing something else," offered the group process consultant.

"You bet your sweet bippy I would!" (Laughter.)

With warmth and empathy the consultant continued, "I more than suspect many of us have been volunteered to this group. Fitting it into our schedules is not going to be easy, so it would be worthwhile to spend some time talking about how we got here."

The managers expressed their anger and annoyance, and they questioned the vagueness of the charge they were given. The group process consultant paraphrased individual members' responses and then summarized what she had heard. She then added, "Since all of us must be on this committee, let's talk about what we can do here to make the time worthwhile."

This proposal led to members' suggestions that perhaps the idea of this group was not so bad, *at least compared to others,* and that maybe some good could come out of it. The end result was that the task was clarified and members agreed to commit to the group for six weeks, at which time they would re-evaluate their work.

Had the group process consultant not developed rapport with the group nor responded to the immediate maintenance needs, the group would have been immediately stuck.

The consultant can expect pressure to direct the group and questions about what to do and how to do it. Empathy with the members and resistance to group pressure are required here. Keep in mind that the consultant's objective, and hopefully the group's, is for members to learn the skills for managing the group toward task accomplishment. In this phase the group process consultant is helping the group set up, through task and maintenance, so they will be equipped to effectively and efficiently approach their major work.

## Consultant Interventions

The commonly used interventions in the setting-up phase are primarily group focused with some interpersonal focus. Cognitive and activity will be the typically selected types with low to moderate intensity. Preferred depth during this stage is Level II. Even with a good contract, members' tolerance for deeper interventions during this phase is low.

The members' behaviors and the consultant's focus indicate why this stage is called the setting-up phase. We gear interventions to create safety and a climate to empower members to work with efficiency and satisfaction. The consultant moves them toward effective work and task skills.

The following are some common consultant task interventions during the setting-up phase:

"What does everyone understand to be the purpose of this group?"

"You might want to assign some roles here, such as time keeper and scribe, which can be rotated through the group."

"Perhaps an agenda would help to set the priority of your work today."

"Before you start to list ideas on the flip chart, you might find it helpful to determine how you wish to proceed."

Common maintenance interventions include:

"How do you feel about being here and working on this project?"

"When I begin a new group like this one, I feel a bit anxious—as I do right now; how about you?"

"How do you feel about your working together, today?"

## WORKING AT AND THROUGH

### General Description

The working-at-and-through phase (Figure 6-3) takes the greatest amount of time in the life of the group. During this major phase the group will reach its level of maturity and complete its charge.

The group settles in. Norms are formed either explicitly or implicitly. With the help of the consultant, members attempt to develop task procedures that will enhance their efficiency and effectiveness. The pressure to conform is strong in the early stages of this phase. However, because of differences in orientations, ideas, and opinions on how to proceed and solve problems, members begin to differentiate, although reluctantly. This differentiation gives rise to a wide range of overt and covert maintenance issues that affect the group. This is seen in behaviors such as resistance to accepting one another's ideas, squabbling over petty issues, power struggles, and apathy.

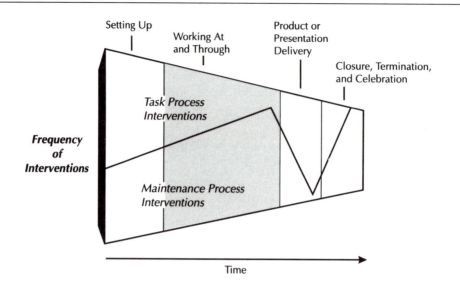

Figure 6-3. Working At and Through

A major issue may arise from the conflict between those who want a high degree of structure and task focus and those who wish time to work on maintenance. Of course, there must be a balance between the two.

Initially, individual needs take precedence over group needs, although the individual needs are not made explicit nor discussed openly. In time, members of successful groups give group needs priority while trying to meet and balance individual needs. As the second phase evolves, the successful group is characterized by risk, support, disclosure, and task experimentation. Creative problem solving becomes the norm.

As in Schutz's (1958) stages of group development, *control* issues emerge. Likewise, Tuckman's (1965) predicted *norming* and *storming* dynamics parallel. Bennis and Shepard's (1948) development subphases, *counterdependence, resolution, enchantment-flight, disenchantment-fight*, and finally, *consensual validation* may unfold during the working-at-and-through phase.

**Task**

The procedural plan in place (setting-up phase), the group now works on fleshing out problem(s) statements and determining data-gathering methods. The group will continue to work through a problem-solving sequence by setting priorities, employing creative problem-solving techniques, selecting options through alternative decision-making strategies, and developing a workable action plan. The group is expected to deliver a specific product or make a presentation. The task focus of the group process consultant will be on the following:

- Problem-solving sequence
- Decision-making strategies
- Use of resources
- Time frames
- Task tracking
- Creative problem-solving techniques

**Maintenance**

The maintenance issues during the working-at-and-through phase emerge rapidly and prolifically. Group members have become more comfortable with themselves. They begin to differentiate. Some members overtly jockey for influence and leadership. Others lay low and work behind the scenes. There is often great intrigue, schemes, conspiracies, and connivances. Although it may sound like the stuff of contemporary fiction, it is normal for all groups or when more than two people get together to solve common problems.

During this phase, now that the group has its procedures and problem-solving mechanisms working relatively well, there is high interaction. High interaction means differences, and differences mean conflict. In this group theater, the group process consultant may feel he or she is simultaneously working multiplays with miniplots and ever-changing scenes. The group members are themselves the authors and actors. Specifically, some of the maintenance areas the consultant can expect to focus on are the following:

- Participation
- Commitment
- Satisfaction
- Maintenance tracking
- Leadership
- Risk taking and challenge
- Competition and comparison to other groups
- Support, encouragement, and affirmation
- Power, control, influence, and pecking order
- Gender, race, and age issues
- Dysfunctional members
- Collaboration
- Members' relationship to authority
- Member autonomy
- Subgrouping
- Conflict and confrontation
- Confidence, esteem, and competence

**Consultant Behaviors**

The group process consultant may find it difficult to keep the group *problem focused* at this time. Groups, teams, and staffs tend to be *solution oriented* and go for the immediate and quick answer. Through focusing and interventions, the group process consultant develops credibility and visibility and becomes a true member of the group, although with a different role. However, after a short period this role difference seems to make little difference to participants and is readily accepted.

**Consultant Interventions**

The working-at-and-through phase will see an increase in maintenance interventions and a decrease in task interventions. That is, once such task issues of procedure, decision making, and data gathering are managed and operational, the group process consultant will focus on making overt those maintenance issues that inhibit or deter the group's work. However, the consultant must not lose sight that *maintenance interventions are always made in the service of the task*. This is true in all four phases, but the focus is critical in the working-at-and-through phase.

In addition to a group intervention focus, the consultant now includes the interpersonal and then the personal foci. Psychological safety has been established. The issues at hand call for interventions with these foci. Intervention types include behavior description and later emotional/reflective. Where it is appropriate, the consultant adds the interpretative.

If an expansive contract has been established, Level-III core issues are accessed in addition to Level II (See Figure 5-4).

At times, where appropriate, Level IV may be probed. For example, a group of senior managers charged themselves with bringing about some dramatic changes in their division. Of the eight managers, two were women. One of the men was Afro-American. There were tight turf boundaries in what they called *silos*. During the initial assessment, group members spoke openly about their problems, including gender and race issues. The group process consultant explained his work and approach and suggested to the group members that if they were serious about dealing with their entire range of issues, they should consider a contract that would legitimize the consultant's making interventions at Levels III and IV when appropriate.

After asking many questions, the members agreed to include that understanding in their contract. Members recognized the importance of maintenance to task and were willing to engage one another. This decision lead to constructive conflict around values and gender and race differences, and subsequently, some creative problem solving was done by the group. Clearly, the education piece and an explicit contract were critical.

As indicated, there is an increased use of maintenance interventions as major socioemotional issues arise. Task interventions are less frequent as the group is well into procedures and has established a decision-making mode and problem-solving activities. However, as the group approaches delivery time, there is a return to task interventions. There are many task details to be monitored and action plans to be made. Presentations require fine tuning; follow-up plans may be required.

---

### Intervention Consideration

*Brainstorming.* Traditional brainstorming may be one of the most misused interventions in the HRD business. Not unlike the *tyranny of the flip chart*, as soon as a group meets, someone suggests, "Let's brainstorm." Even members who have been working together for some time may have difficulty in brainstorming *as a group*. Members feel the pressure of performance, censure, and tacit evaluation. Consider, instead, brainstorming individually and then offering the items—one from each person via the nominal group technique, that is, round robin. The group members will probably find it far more effective.

Another technique is to individually write single items on 3" x 5" index cards. Toss the cards anonymously in the center of the table. Group members reach in and draw a card. Upon seeing what is written they add another item triggered by the first. The card is returned and the process continues until the cards are exhausted.

---

## PRODUCT OR PRESENTATION DELIVERY

### General Description

The third phase is characterized by much task activity as members put final touches on their project or presentation (Figure 6-4). As one member somewhat indelicately stated, "We were like a bunch of rats running around!" Later when pushed, he added, "Oh, yes, we knew what we were doing; it was pretty exciting." This phase is *very* task focused. There is little tolerance for maintenance issues. Moreover, conformity pressures increase dramatically. When maintenance issues of importance arise—and they will—the group process consultant must assert himself or herself to have members confront the issues.

Tuckman's (1965) *performing* dynamics are readily seen in this phase. That is, group cohesiveness is in evidence and group members are more comfortable in working with one another despite now obvious differences. Group needs take precedence over individuals' needs, and members express fewer negative opinions toward the offerings of others.

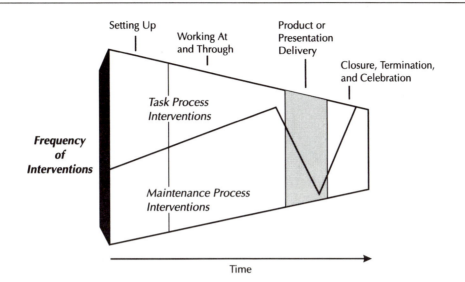

Setting Up

Working At
and Through

Product or
Presentation
Delivery

Closure, Termination,
and Celebration

*Task Process
Interventions*

***Frequency
of
Interventions***

*Maintenance Process
Interventions*

Time

**Figure 6-4. Product or Presentation Delivery**

---

**Task**

As the following specifics suggest, there are many "details" about which the group members must think, and—most importantly—act on:

- Situation politics
- Presentation details
- Project completion
- Meeting deadlines
- Involving ancillary resources
- Room setup and configuration
- Who will do what when

**Maintenance**

The maintenance dynamics during this phase tend to be less obvious than in the first two phases. They also include political issues (e.g., who is to receive the report) and how the group's work will be viewed by others. Some of the specific dynamics to be focused on during the product-or-presentation-delivery phase include the following:

- Premature closure
- Presentation anxiety
- Perception of managers who are receiving completed work
- Irritability around how to do details
- Group and individual competence
- Intergroup and intragroup competition
- Who is contributing what
- Commitment to final product
- Staying power of members

## Consultant Behavior

The above-mentioned frenetic behavior is typical during this brief phase of work-group activity. This is what the group process consultant will need to manage; that is, keep the energy, motivation, and striving for excellence, yet see to it that the task bases are covered and that no major maintenance issues are suppressed in such a way that they might later destructively emerge.

It is easy for the group process consultant to get pulled into the content during this phase. The group process consultant has been a member of the group and is committed to the outcome. Given his or her position and role, he or she can place a strong influence on the group regarding its product.

## Consultant Interventions

At this point in the life of the group, the group process consultant—given he or she has the contract—is intervening at all depths and using whatever interventions are necessary. The greatest challenge is to help keep the group on task, yet not ignore critical maintenance issues. There may also be a tendency for some group members to move impulsively on decisions without thinking through the implications.

Periodic stops with "Let me do a quick check on how you feel you are doing at this point" are very helpful. The members respond and the work continues, unless a group member raises an issue. Sometimes it is thought that this quick intervention can slow down the group. If a group is operating efficiently and effectively, quick maintenance checks will not slow it down; indeed, long breaks tend not to inhibit the effective or high-performing group.

The action is fast and the group process consultant must work to stay on top of the action. He or she needs to be relevant, on target, and not intrusive—not an easy job.

Some interventions to consider are the following:

"Is it clear to everyone who is doing what?"

"It strikes me that the group has been moving very quickly to decision; has everyone really bought in?"

"Perhaps you might consider a contingency plan in case something goes awry."

"Let me do a quick check here on how optimistic or pessimistic you are about the outcome."

"Where are you with the group's level of creativity? Do you think you are pushing yourselves hard enough?"

## CLOSURE, TERMINATION, AND CELEBRATION

### General Description

As the group winds down after delivering its product or making its presentation, it reflects on its history (Figure 6-5). Members evaluate accomplishments, contributions, and satisfactions. With the help of the consultant, members also discuss issues and concerns about termination. The consultant must help the group bring closure to its tenure. Final tasks and action steps are taken. The time and appropriate manner to celebrate the group's accomplishments and relationships should be established. All too frequently this important aspect of the group is ignored, avoided, or dismissed. Yet, celebration helps bring positive closure to the group's life.

With the help of a group process consultant, the group has completed its work to some level of satisfaction. Morale is usually quite high. Members may tend to be a little cocky about their achievements. There is a feeling of teamwork, cohesion, and unity. Indeed, one potential concern here is if the group members are to continue working together, they may have become

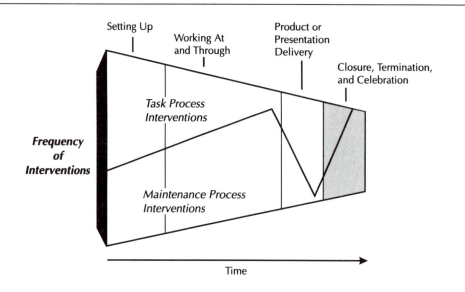

**Figure 6-5. Closure, Termination, and Celebration**

too insular. That is, they may tend to resist or reject input or scrutiny from the outside.

Feelings of affiliation and affection surface—and can be quite uncomfortable for some group members. Disclosure and discussion about feelings in general and affection in particular continue to be verboten in many corporate cultures, especially in North America. Yet, when group members have struggled to-gether on a project and—with the help of the group process consultant—have disclosed, confronted, risked, been creative, worked long hours, and put group before individual needs, there is bound to be closeness. This is characteristic of high-performing groups and teams. Together members have attained a commit-ment to the project—and to one another.

"Could I have done more? Did I *really* contribute to the success of this project?" These and similar questions may be on the minds of members at this time.

Dynamics around Schutz's (1958) stage of *affection* emerge during this final phase. Rather than disclose directly feelings of affection, members will substitute *cohesion* or describe friendships they have developed. The words *bonding* and *closeness* are sometimes used to convey affection. In one case, a rather gruff senior vice president said the executive team reminded him of his youth in the boy scouts at the end of a camping trip. The group process consultant asked him to describe the similarity in experience and feelings. The VP talked wistfully about camaraderie, sharing, and closeness, then exclaimed, "My god, that's what we have here!"

## Task

The task dynamics in this phase, unlike other phases, grow out of the maintenance issues around closure, termination, and celebration. In other phases, maintenance dynamics grow out of task demands.

In the fourth phase there may also be a question of the group's expanding its scope and working on new projects together. This is particularly true if the group has been highly successful. The group process consultant can help to determine if this desire to continue is realistic or related only to the recent experience. Thus, the group process consultant must explore both task and maintenance dynamics. He or she may have to be particularly aware of the boundary between task process and content. The idea here is to suggest the areas and how to work them versus giving advice or filling in the content.

Specific focal task themes in this phase include:

- Final tasks to be completed
- Who should be informed about what
- Publicity
- Reports
- Evaluation of team performance
- Task elements of the celebration

## Maintenance

This final phase of work-group activity is primarily one of maintenance. Although there are a few task dynamics on which to focus, the majority of interventions have to do with feelings around work, interpersonal relationships, and closing down the group. It is not unusual for some members to withdraw from the group as a way of defending against anxiety about separating.

The group process consultant may have to challenge the group if they distort and overestimate their accomplishments and potential to again work together. This is a delicate area as you do not want to devalue the group's work but just bring in a bit of reality.

Specifically, the group process consultant will target the following maintenance areas in his or her interventions:

- Members' feelings about the group and what the group accomplished
- Members' feelings about their own contributions
- What was learned, positive and negative
- Cohesion
- Termination
- Loss
- Sadness
- Elation
- Anger
- Friendship
- Intimacy
- Prides and regrets over the life of the group
- Celebration
- Good-byes

**Consultant Behavior**

The frequency of the group process consultant's interventions has lessened considerably from the initial phases. Moreover, the group members are accustomed to the nature of the interventions and provide many themselves, although typically not at deep levels. During this final phase, however, the nature of the interventions is different from those previously made. The project is over; the delivery made; the presentation offered. The group process consultant now focuses on a review of the task and maintenance processes. The intent is not to lay blame for mistakes but instead to ferret out task lessons learned and arrange for transfer of training to new tasks. Remember a metagoal of group process consultation is that members are able to work together more effectively in the future.

On the maintenance side, the focus will be on how group members feel about their accomplishments and working with one another. Also to be considered, and as important, is how members feel about ending the project and their time spent together. It is important to discuss feelings about closure and ending the group. The feelings range from elation to sadness. Members need to understand that these feelings are normal and expected.

Finally, the group process consultant can raise the question of how the group should celebrate its work, life together, and ending. Supposedly, the consultant has raised the affirmation and celebration questions throughout the life of the group.

---

### Intervention Consideration

*Formal Check-In.* In the formal check-in, participants sit in a circle with the group process consultant. All members are asked to comment on where they are in their relation to the group or on their view of group effectiveness, group dynamics, and so on. The intent is to generate simple statements that will capture the pulse of the group. Most important, no comment may be *rebutted;* that is, members' statements and questions are simply offered for all to hear. Questions are not asked nor comments made about these statements. It is a very freeing experience.

---

## Consultant Interventions

The interventions during this final phase, particularly maintenance, need to reflect a good deal of sensitivity. Group members are often loath to share feelings around closeness, camaraderie, and affiliation.

A middle manager had seen his team through difficult times and was respected and liked by group members. However, as the group expressed their affection for him, he became obviously uncomfortable and said little. The following session he was unusually quiet and contributed minimally. The group process consultant asked what was going on, to which he received little response. The consultant wisely suggested that perhaps the manager's silence was related to the positive feedback and affection he received during the previous session. The manager reluctantly agreed and commented that the expression of affection in the workplace was questionable. He related that when given the feedback, he felt vulnerable and not in control, hence incompetent.

The group members explained that indeed his vulnerability made him seem more competent and that their feedback and affection was a way of saying "thank you." The exchange had a powerful effect on the manager who confessed he had never been involved in such a discussion.

At the next session he returned to the group with renewed energy and maximal contributions. Had the group process consultant been insensitive to or uncomfortable in this area, neither the manager nor the group would have benefited nor the task effectiveness enhanced.

The group process consultant may have to use himself or herself in generating discussion about closure: "At times like this, after I've worked with a group for a while, I find it difficult to break away—just to pack up and leave. I suspect I'm not the only one feeling this way."

Still another intervention is to urge the group to examine its work together, so members can pull out some principles: "It might be valuable to spend some talking about how you feel about what you've accomplished here and in working with one another."

Focusing on task accomplishment can be aided by having the group members review their time together in terms of what they are proud of and what they regret. Regarding separation anxiety, the group process consultant might offer, "It's common for group members to feel a bit anxious about ending a group; sometimes it's easier just to back off. I wonder if that might be happening here."

You may have to describe the value of celebrating and how it relates to bringing the group to a close. In addition, you can offer ideas regarding celebration and affirmation as well as have the group generate its own. A few celebration ideas the group may consider are the following:

- Newsletter kudos
- Photo displays
- Meeting with upper management
- Team-appreciation day
- Group dinner
- Artistically designed memento
- Trophies
- Public acknowledgement by executives
- Sports events
- Time off
- Travel
- T-shirts and logos
- Recognition boutonniere
- Public affirmation of each person's contribution

---

### Intervention Consideration

*Describe Your Group.* "You are in a closed room with your best friend and confidant. How would you describe this group and its dynamics to that person?"

Often group members have strong feelings about their group or team but are reluctant to express those feelings publicly. In addition, they have insightful perceptions of the group dynamics. A simple but effective intervention is to ask group members to close their eyes and respond to the above direction.

**SUMMARY**

This chapter has offered a range of interventions through the phases of work-group activity. I have suggested a few from countless others. Each group is different and its dynamics unique. Perhaps all group process consultants know this, but regardless of how on-target your interventions and your commitment to the process are, *some groups just do not work!* The reasons are many and varied.

The availability of a group process consultant can certainly help overcome issues that the group by itself could not. Group process consultants sometimes blame themselves when a group is not effective; yet, the control over the group for direction and learning is, at best, limited. Despite the competence, education, training, and experience of the group process consultant, there is a harsh reality and truth in the adage "A group is as good as its weakest member."

In many of the groups with which we will work, there are members who are resistive, rigid, unwilling to cooperate, counter-dependent, and may have characterological personality problems. The impact on the effectiveness of the group is negative at best and devastating at worse. Most often this can be avoided by educating, assessing, and having a good contract with the group. If the group process consultant's self-esteem is contingent on the success of every group to which he or she consults, that consultant may well be in the wrong profession.

Chapter Seven articulates and examines the capacities that lead to becoming a competent, balanced, and effective group process consultant.

## Executive Planning Team ♦ ♦ ♦

As the executive team continued to work, power struggles developed over who should be doing what and who would be the recipient of what resources. Scott found himself intervening at deeper levels in an attempt to surface the dynamics issues. Some group members balked at his interventions as irrelevant.

Scott decided to renegotiate his contract. He explained why he was making the interventions and their value. Because group members had agreed they wanted to be a high-performing team, intense interaction, confrontation, and conflict around ideas were all necessary. The group members agreed and then re-explored their original work norms to include the new behaviors. In addition, Scott offered an array of creative problem-solving activities from which the group could draw. The new norms agreement and idea-generating methods were major breakthroughs. Members would brainstorm ideas uncritically and during the evaluation phase challenge each other with great intensity. They reveled in their creative ideas yet continued to have difficulty in collaborating on selected solutions.

## Quality Circles ♦ ♦ ♦

*Circle I.* Circle I members came to the session ready to work the issues they had prioritized the previous week. Kim suggested they might wish to spend some time on each of the items of competition, ownership, and uneven contribution. As soon as they agreed, Phil launched into his concerns about competition within the circle and with Circles II and III. Phil acknowledged his striving to be "one up." As a result of this disclosure, all members spoke of their "competitive nature," as Zeb called it.

Recognizing there was more to discuss on the competition issue, Kim checked to see if the group wished to move on to explore ownership and uneven contribution. Members decided the two concerns were related and should be discussed together. The remainder of the session was intense. Kim pushed for clarity, summarized, and requested paraphrases. Time passed quickly. Kim interrupted the discussion ten minutes before the end of the session and asked how members felt about their work that day.

"I can't believe we actually did it," said an elated Phil.

"Next step?" asked Kim.

The group agreed to return to task next session. Members reemphasized Kim's value in *calling the game* in her role as group process consultant.

*Circle II.* Michael arrived at Circle II's next session prepared to recontract with the group. Although he really had nothing new to add to his original contract, it did afford an opportunity to discuss his and circle members' expectations and how deeply Michael might intervene. After the discussion, Michael felt he now had legitimacy and credibility to intervene wherever and however he thought appropriate.

Michael also used this discussion to indicate that he saw a group need for additional creative problem-solving techniques. At this point Circle II was limited in its creative problem-solving repertoire. With alacrity Circle II members agreed and requested training.

*Circle III.* His meeting with the human resources manager was not to Larry's liking. Sharon, the manager, tried to get Larry to look at his behavior as group process consultant and not just at the participants' behavior.

Larry resisted, stating, "If they'd only do what I tell them, they wouldn't have half these problems."

Sharon suggested Larry meet with Circle III and confront the maintenance issues. Larry reluctantly agreed, thinking it would be a waste of time.

At the next session of Circle III, Larry alluded to the 65-percent attendance: "Our sponsor thinks things aren't going too well. She wants to know what's up."

Members reacted either with apathy or mild annoyance: "Who told Sharon we weren't doing so good?"

Larry responded, "I had a meeting with her."

"Why didn't you ask us about this first?"

"I tried, but nobody was interested."

Jason interrupted. "Hey, look; this is just a lot of bull. We're almost done with our work here; let's move on."

With a few head nods and no further comments from Larry, Circle III pushed ahead on task.

## Hospital Administration ♦ ♦ ♦

So the group would not get bogged down in maintenance issues to the exclusion of task, as they had previously, Laura intervened frequently and appropriately. Knowing that the group was also lacking in task process skills, Laura reduced process loss by suggesting task structure and focusing the group on its work. Even the maintenance discussions were bounded or focused. For example, Laura suggested a discussion around roles, formal and informal. The formal roles were expected to be easier to discuss than informal roles. However, because of an overlap in responsibility and authority, turf issues became paramount.

Laura suggested the group might continue its planning and later return to the issue of roles as it became more relevant to the plan. Members supported the suggestion, both because they thought it correct and, also, because most did not yet want to deal with that conflict now that they were getting some work accomplished.

Lucia, the director of nursing, was increasingly disruptive. She spoke loudly, was aggressive, and arrogantly stated that only she knew what really was going on in the hospital. She sneered at what others offered. Her dysfunctional behavior seemed to increase when Laura attempted to refocus the group on task. During one session, after Laura had intervened, Lucia stated that following the task process was a waste of time. "We should just sit down and work things out."

Other members visibly backed off. Laura addressed Lucia: "When that was attempted earlier, it didn't seem to work out. The group felt it didn't have the skill to deal with conflict or intense emotion. Is it different now?"

Jeremy offered, "We still aren't quite ready to deal with one another."

Lucia retorted, "If you don't have the guts for a little straight talk, that's too bad."

Jeremy flushed and looked down.

Laura responded, "Lucia, if I had been on the receiving end of that comment, I'd feel put down, angry, and upset."

Lucia shrugged, "I didn't say it to you."

Jeremy then responded, "No, you said it to me, and I feel like Laura said."

Laura intervened, "Which is...?"

Jeremy said, "Frankly, I'm pissed. I think one of the reasons we have so much difficulty with conflict, Lucia, is your behavior.

You are always putting somebody down...just like me a minute ago. Usually, I don't say anything, but this time Laura made it easier for me to speak my mind."

Lucia began to defend her position.

Laura interrupted with "Let me suggest before you begin that you check out Jeremy's perception. Would you like to know where other folks are?"

Lucia agreed to listen to the feedback. In turn the other members told Lucia how she came across and how intimidated they felt. Some members acknowledged their own responsibility in letting Lucia control the group. Others only described her behavior. Laura checked with Lucia periodically to see if the feedback was helpful and whether she wanted to continue. She affirmed each.

Then Laura asked, "Lucia, what do you hear people telling you?"

Lucia replied, "Wow, I had no idea I was coming on that strong. I should have guessed something, since my mouth has got me in trouble before. I am just so tired of wasting time on what I consider to be trivia. And no one wants to engage anyone."

Laura asked the group, "Where are the rest of you on this?"

For the first time, group members began to discuss their own fear of confrontation and the consequent bogged-down state. Slowly it became clear that Lucia was a mouthpiece for the group's frustrations. The discussion had a freeing effect on the members as they regrouped and discussed ways of moving forward. As the session ended, they agreed to pick up the discussion at their next meeting.

# Group Process Consultant Competencies

**7**

*C*<sub></sub>*an* anyone become a group process consultant? Technically, the answer, of course, is yes. Can anyone become an *effective* process consultant? The answer is at least questionable, if not an outright no. This chapter explores the consultant's role and competencies. In conclusion, the group process consultant will be urged to create a personal developmental plan for further training, practice, and experience.

## TASK DIMENSIONS

Returning to the initial question, "Can anyone become a group process consultant?" people certainly can be trained to conduct process consultation. As one might guess, the training most easily learned is around the task dimension. Indeed, this has been one of the problems in the field. Often consultants—both external and internal—with minimal training in group dynamics and maintenance interventions and, at best, possessing a modicum of interpersonal skills set themselves up as "process experts." Yet, their only focus has been task. When the group bogs down as a result of conflict or other interpersonal and maintenance dynamics, the consultant is not equipped to manage the situation.

A high percentage of group failures, and this includes task forces, teams, quality circles, and ad hoc groups, are probably a result of inadequate training, lack of understanding of the need for group maintenance, and interpersonal ineptness on the consultant's part. Little practitioner screening, if any, is done, and there is no licensure nor true certification.

Currently, it seems that everyone is becoming an organizational or human resources consultant. Within these two categories, people with little or no training are called on to conduct process consultations. We often hear stories such as "Yesterday, I was an engineer. I was about to be laid off because of downsizing, then management asked me if I wanted to work with and facilitate groups in HRD."

Does the reverse happen? That is, are human resources personnel asked to take a position in engineering? The mind set is that anyone can effectively deal with human relations and group dynamics. In actuality, human behavior and group dynamics are far more complex than most other fields and at least as complex as engineering! Because everyone has "feelings" and is engaged in social interactions, many people think of themselves as *de facto* "experts."

Recently, I have been appalled at hearing of so-called group specialists who after a *year or less* of didactic training are in the field primarily as independent practitioners, conducting workshops, leading small groups, or consulting to organizations. Sadly, we are in an era when many people in professional fields wish to possess the title "consultant." Whether it is a fantasy of money or prestige, the consultant of today is "developed" in a few months versus years—and without first serving in an apprentice model that includes intensive supervision (Reddy, 1985, p. 106).

Over fifteen years ago, Harry Levinson (1977) wrote:

I think you have to build into organizations an increasing awareness among managers of the complexities they are dealing with. There has been a lot of talk in business about being practical, hard-nosed. We're warned not to get long-haired, not to get abstract and more complex. But the more complex it becomes, the more abstract your basis of knowledge has to become. You can't expect a tinkerer who fixes a model T to be equally effective in handling the problems of a space machine.

## FOUR MAJOR COMPETENCIES

What should the group process consultant know? This chapter we examines group process consultant competencies, what they are, and how they can be acquired.

Figure 7-1 illustrates the four major competencies required of an effective group process consultant, namely, *theory, behavioral skills, intervention skills,* and *self-knowledge.* In turn, theory is divided into *learning, change, group dynamics, group process consultation,* and *evaluation.* Under behavioral skills we explore *contracting, observation, training, structure,* and *assessment.* Intervention skills include *task* and *maintenance areas* and *conflict management.* The last major area, self-knowledge, includes *personal development, values, style, giving and receiving feedback,*

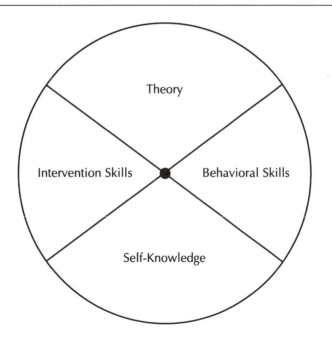

**Figure 7-1. Wheel of Competencies**

*managing diversity, strengths and limitations, gender,* and *intuition.*

The relative size of the divisions in Figure 7-1 do not represent relative importance nor priority. However, I personally believe self-knowledge is the most critical in group process consultation.

## THEORY

We will examine five competencies in this major group.

### Learning Theory

Group process consultants need to know generally how people learn, how people in groups learn, and how people learn in groups. There are over a hundred years of research on learning. While the practitioner does not need an in-depth knowledge of learning theory, there is value in knowing critical factors such as massed versus spaced learning, optimal learning conditions, and learning curves (Zechmeister & Nyberg, 1982), as well as such approaches as modeling and reinforcement.

### Change Theory

Related to learning, yet more behavioral, what are the conditions that must operate before people are willing to change their behavior? Schein (1961) describes three stages of interpersonal change: unfreezing, changing, and refreezing. He emphasizes that the individual may have to unlearn before he or she can relearn. Thus, the group member may have to undergo disconfirmation via feedback before he or she changes behaviors to those that are more effective.

Ackerman (1986) speaks of developmental, transitional, and transformational change. Developmental change focuses on improving of what already exists. Transitional change targets a known or agreed-on end point and over a managed period of time moves to that point. Transformational change is movement into the unknown. The shape of the new state is emergent and typically evolves out of the termination, often chaotic, of a former state. Unlike developmental change and transitional change, managing or controlling time in transformational change is at best very difficult.

How does this relate to the small group or team? In discussing its objectives and vision, the group process consultant can help the team determine where it wants to go, what it wishes to change, and what strategies are available to get there.

The implication from these theories is that the group process consultant needs to plan what kind of change is required for effective work and how interventions and feedback can best lead to that change.

## Group Dynamics

As strange as it may sound, I meet countless practitioners each year who have not had training, course, nor text on group dynamics. Their belief is "What you see is all there is." As we have discussed, there is more than overt behavior. There are many fine university courses available on group dynamics. In addition, among the many excellent texts are Tubbs (1992), Forsyth (1990), and Shaw (1981). Content areas typically covered include group formation, physical environment, development, socialization, structure, composition, personal characteristics, leadership, conflict, change, problem solving and decision making, effectiveness, and communication processes.

---

### Intervention Consideration

*Words Used to Express Emotions.*
1. "I think maybe I'm angry."
2. "I think I'm angry."
3. "I think I feel angry."
4. "I feel angry."
5. "I'm angry."
6. "Damn!"

Listen carefully to the words group members use in expressing emotions. The first three examples above describe feelings as thoughts. The second three are successively more direct in expression. By using the numbers from 1 to 6, the consultant can quantify the depth of group and individual emotional expression.

---

## Dynamics Specific to Group Process Consultation

There are conceptual areas specific to group process consultation that should be known by the practitioner, namely, flow of process consultation, contracting, task/maintenance processes, and intervention type, focus, intensity, and depth. Earlier chapters have dealt at length in these areas; the importance I place on them is obvious.

## Evaluation

Although the group process consultant is usually not called on to formally evaluate the group's progress toward goal completion, he or she may need to evaluate progress for his or her own understanding of the group. Goal criteria, task progress, and milestones are also used as bench marks for interventions. The evaluation work of Goodstein & Goodstein (1991), Grove & Ostroff (1990), and Kirkpatrick (1959, 1960) are particularly useful. Kirkpatrick (1967) states that several conditions must exist for the participant to benefit from training. These conditions are necessary for a team of group members:

1. The group member will need to have the opportunity to use and practice the learning—and with the encouragement of supervisors.

2. The application of the learning must be seen as related to work efficiency.

3. The participant must be committed to improving work performance.

Patton (1981) offers "A Beginning List of Alphabet Soup Approaches to Evaluation." There are 132 specific approaches in this remarkable *beginning* list from *Accessibility focus* to *Norm-referenced focus* to *Zounds approach*!

There is a second, ongoing, evaluation; that is, "How effectively is the group process consultant working with the group? Is the consultant modeling effective behaviors? Are members themselves executing task and maintenance processes?" Conversely, if members are not tracking well or if they totally rely on the consultant's interventions, the consultant needs to review the dimensions of effective consultation and use the evaluation criteria. A *formal check-in*, (see Chapter Six) suggested by the consultant, will give participants the opportunity to share their thoughts and feelings about the consultation without having to defend their comments.

## BEHAVIORAL SKILLS

Although the consultant may have well-ingrained group process consultation theory and concepts, he or she also needs a set of behavioral skills in contracting, observation, and training.

## Contracting

Contracting is both an important concept and a critical skill. We need to understand the notion of contracting and the management of boundaries. Consultants must also be able to negotiate a group contract in such a way that members feel empowered and psychologically safe. It is not easy. Contracting demands skill, empathy, and much practice. McGonagle's (1981, 1982) texts on formal contracting are worth reading. McGonagle (1981) offers twelve guideline areas and suggests that they can be covered in contracts in as many paragraphs:

1. Terms of the Agreement Including Time Line,
2. Nature of the Consultant's Activities,
3. Remuneration Details and Schedule,
4. Work Facilities,
5. Reports and Expected Products,
6. Expectations of Consultant as an Independent Contractor,
7. Termination Understanding,
8. Confidentiality,
9. Accountability and Subcontracting,
10. Managing Disputes,
11. Changing the Contract, and
12. Closing and Signing the Contract.

## Observation

One the best ways to learn is to observe groups in action. This can be done in the natural setting or via video tape—which can be stopped, replayed, and discussed without disrupting the group. Observers can be trained regarding what to observe (Hanson, 1972; McCall & Simmons, 1969; Simon & Boyer, 1974) and to code interactions (Bales & Cohen, 1979). For example, areas to focus on include the following: who is talking to whom and how often; who is high or low on influence; what operating values are driving the group; what the group climate is; whether subgroups are forming; who is supporting whom; what decision-making processes the group has adopted and whether a decision was implicit or explicit; and what norms have evolved around attendance, conflict, communication, gender, and race.

## Training

Group process consultants are sometimes called on to intervene at an activities/skills level or to present didactic information. Presentation and training knowledge, skills, and experience are essential. Moreover, group process consultants who have training skills maintain a "kit bag" of activities, exercises, and techniques to pull out when needed. These include icebreakers, a problem-solving format and creative problem-solving techniques, brief conceptual inputs, communication skills such as paraphrasing, and ways of managing conflict. Training skills are also needed when the consultant is called on to "sell" group process consultation to an organization or unit. When is it appropriate to sit or stand? Is it advantageous to use overheads slides, or a flip chart? The ability to project oneself and develop good platform skills are valuable assets. Kelley (1975) offers these design and style considerations in critiquing a training session.[1]

Design Considerations:

1. Goals and Preparation

2. Directions

3. Lecturettes

---

[1] From "Guidelines for Critiquing a Training Presentation" by C.A. Kelley, 1975, *Small-Group Training Theory and Practice: Workshop Participant Book*. San Diego, CA: Pfeiffer & Company. Used with permission.

4. Processing

5. Time Limits

6. Staging

7. Participants and Staff

8. Materials

9. Design and Atmosphere

Style Considerations:

1. Voice

2. Verbal Behavior

3. Interventions

4. Co-facilitation

## Structure

In most organizations, there will be little opportunity to work in a purely unstructured group setting such as T-groups or sensitivity training. However, training and practice sessions in such quasi-unstructured groups is invaluable. The tasks may be ambiguous. The void created by the ambiguity is filled by members' behaviors and utterances. Group dynamics emerge in caricature and thus are more easily decipherable. Indeed, it is a wonderful way to learn about groups and group dynamics, and there is transfer to the back-home setting. Although we tend not to work with totally unstructured groups on the job, many of the issues, problems, and concerns of organizational groups are quite ambiguous. The dynamics of the back-home group are the same as those more easily seen in the "practice" group.

Most internal and external consultants work in structured group settings. That is, the general charge, task, objectives, or goals of the group are known as are basic expectations, such as projected task completion. There is much information available about the dynamics of structured groups, phases, communications, problem solving, and so on. Keeping a journal or log while one is in or observing a group can be invaluable to understanding the group and one's role in the group.

## Assessment

I've been impressed with clinical psychologists who have become group process consultants. Their early training includes assessment theory, psychometrics, interview skills, and intervention practice. Although initially they may lack *group* intervention skills, they are typically adept at assessing individuals and groups as well as developing *individual* intervention skills. Assessment, individual and group, is a group process consultant competency that requires interviewing skills and knowledge and use of instruments. As explored in an earlier section, group assessment can be approached traditionally, focused on individual members and through survey and personality instruments. The group can also be assessed via a more contemporary approach, that is, through the group itself with all members present and generating a common data base (Reddy & Phillips, 1992). We will again briefly look at the two approaches.

### Group Assessment via the Individual

*Interviewing.* The most effective way to learn one-on-one interviewing is to interview under supervision and with video tape. One, of course, needs to know what to look for, how to structure the interview, how to draw out the interviewee, and, most importantly, how to establish rapport (Dexter, 1970). Basic communication skills of accurate empathy, questioning, and paraphrasing must be learned. One needs a framework in which to place the data gleaned and to be prepared to share the information in understandable dynamic terms to the group. Writing skills are also essential, as one is frequently asked to submit a formal report for the group.

*Instruments.* There are many group, team, and individual instruments available that will help the practitioner assess group functioning (Pfeiffer, Heslin, & Jones, 1973). Some are global and pick up general themes or dysfunctional aspects of the group. Others are quite specific and focus on creativity, conflict, communication, decision making, and so on.

A major difficulty is knowing whether these are valid instruments. Many, perhaps the majority, are neither valid nor reliable. Some instruments are produced with the sole purpose of monetary gain. That is, the instruments are used as items for sale or as marketing tools. Increasingly, we see the three-day certification program for "Instrument Z." Although some certification programs are useful and protective of both client and practitioners, others are a means to pressure and control practitioners in the use a particular instrument. If a group process consultant is serious about the use of instruments, there are courses and readings available on tests, test construction, and psychometrics. Tests, measures, and instruments are big business in group work, organization development, and training. Unfortunately, some popular instruments, such as the Myers-Briggs Type Indicator (MBTI), have gravitated to pop psychology and faddism. The human personality is a bit more complex than to reduce a person to a four-letter label. Luft, Kingsbury, and Schrader (1990) decry this situation. They point out the general misuse of psychometrics, and the MBTI in particular, stressing its weak validity and inadequate research and the current faddism, overuse, and poorly trained practitioners. The National Research Council's Committee on Techniques for the Enhancement of Human Performance (1991) has also challenged the use of the MBTI in career-counseling programs: "At this time there is not sufficient well-designed research to justify the use of the Myers-Briggs Type Indicator.... Much of the current evidence is based on inadequate methodologies" (p. 15).

*Group Assessment via the Group*

Chapter Three examined the advantages and disadvantages of traditional assessment and the promise that group assessment holds. Many individual techniques can be implemented in group assessment.

*Interviews.* If all members agree, the entire group can be interviewed. There are many permutations to this approach. That is, the consultant can interview individuals, pairs, or trios, while the rest of the group observes. In one assessment, members interviewed each other in dyads and reported the data back to the total group.

With a good client-consultant contract and a strong manager and group, an empty chair (representing the manager) can be placed in the center of the room. In actuality, he or she sits off to the side listening. The group members share their concerns, apprehensions, and issues with the symbolic chair. The manager listens while the data are generated. As in other formats, they are limited only by the constraints put on by the group process consultant and the group members themselves.

*Instruments.* As with interviews, paper-and-pencil instruments can be used in a group setting. Although in some instances the psychometrics and standardization of the instrument may be violated, what is gained are members' discussions of issues interactively. For example, the consultant can ask specific instrument questions of the entire group, and the group tries to reach consensus on the answers. The method generates much discussion and, again, builds that common data base.

If group members individually complete an instrument, the consultant must be prepared to discuss the results immediately with the group. Subgroups can be formed and given different data-generating tasks and consequent action steps. As always, the data and suggested action steps are shared. These methods are truly *action research* at its best. That is, as soon as the data are generated, they are shared and used to understand and to define the issues and then to generate tentative actions.

## Ongoing Assessment

The group process consultant is continually assessing dynamics—at a group level, interpersonal level, and personal level—as the group works. The consultant must be aware of individual behaviors—committed or omitted—patterns, and dynamics. Chapter Five introduced the "Ten Clues" assessment form. Over time, the group process consultant imprints these and other clues on which to focus. Likewise, the consultant senses and explicates the incongruities between what group members or the group norms say and how consistent their behavior is.

## INTERVENTION SKILLS

These skills include task and maintenance areas and conflict management.

## Task

Sometimes novices think that working a group is all maintenance. They shun learning or using tools that have been around for a long time and have proven valuable. There are six major task areas and sets of techniques the group process consultant might include in the "kit bag":

1. Vision, mission, objectives
2. Decision-making strategies
3. Problem-solving sequence
4. Data-gathering and prioritization techniques
5. Creative problem-solving techniques
6. Conflict management

## Vision, Mission, Objectives

Groups need to determine who they are, where they want to go, their reason for being, and how they can reach their objectives. The group process consultant can aid in that process if he or she knows the technology and techniques in creating a vision, determining a mission, and setting objectives. Although much has been written on the subject, Peter Block's (1987) articulation is particularly useful, as is that by Goodstein, Nolan, and Pfeiffer (1992).

## Decision-Making Strategies

Since the onset of employee involvement, quality circles, and the team concept, there has been a mindset that *all* decisions must be made by consensus. Although consensus is a valuable approach, it is best limited to problems in which both quality and acceptance are required (Maier, 1963). Majority voting, multiple voting, expert decision, and fairness determinants all have their place (Fisher, 1974).

Even in situations where consensus is appropriate, there are variations. For example, it is not unusual for one or two resistive or counter-dependent group members to consistently block the group from making decisions by consensus. An inordinate amount of time can be used up—if not wasted—in trying to reach consensus. A strategy used by some groups is to limit the amount of time spent on a particular discussion. Consensus is attempted. If it cannot be reached by the set time, the group votes by a set quorum, typically 75 percent of its members. This technique has proven very successful.

## Problem-Solving Sequence

There are many structured problem-solving sequences available, some left-brained oriented, others right, some prescriptive, others descriptive (Tubbs, 1992). The group process consultant needs to have these task interventions to draw on. Many groups are ineffective simply because members have no tools with which to work. The idea of defining a problem first, as elementary as that sounds, may be unknown to the untrained. The fundamental problem-solving sequence usually includes at least six basic steps:

1. Problem identification, statement, and description;
2. Problem analysis via a force field;
3. Data gathering for action alternatives;
4. Designing plans for action;
5. Simulating the plan for strengths and flaws; and
6. Initiating and operationalizing the plan.

## Data-Gathering and Prioritization Techniques

Task forces, work-group committees, teams, ad hoc groups, and quality circles typically gather data and information to solve the issues and problems on which they are working. The information is then placed in a hierarchy of importance or priority. The expertise of the group process consultant is to *suggest* how they might go about that task.

Too many consultants inappropriately use brainstorming as their only data-gathering technique. Brainstorming (Osborne, 1963) was created to generate a quantity of ideas. Quality follows quality. Once ideas are generated individually, they are shared *publicly* in *nominal-group* fashion, that is, round robin. Members are encouraged to add new items as they are stimulated by other ideas generated. Evaluation, of course, comes later. What has evolved in our task-and-results oriented organizations is the technique of *group brainstorming*. Of course, the dynamics, pressures, and constraints found in all groups are present. Quantity is less and quality reduced (Dunnette, Campbell, & Jaastad, 1963; Bouchard, 1972).

Data-generating techniques such as interviews, surveys, and focused instruments (Dunham & Smith, 1979; Nadler, 1977) should also be available to the effective group process consultant.

The use of multi-voting reduces process loss and speeds prioritization. Each group member can be given three colored signal dots and asked to make his or her priority selection. This can be done repeatedly until the group has a *workable* number of items. It does not mean all items not selected are unimportant. It does help to reduce the number, so they can be worked on by the group.

*Creative
Problem-Solving
Techniques*

For highly interacting groups and teams working on the front edge of their organizations, there are equally leading-edge creative problem-solving techniques available to the group process consultant (Fox, 1987; Michalko, 1991; VanGundy, 1981).

One of my now favorite techniques is offered by Michalko (1991), building on the work of Alex Osborn and Robert Eberle. It is called *SCAMPER* and it can be used with most other problem-solving techniques. At decision points in any creative problem-solving technique consider the following questions:

1. What can be *substituted (S)*?
2. What can I *combine (C)*?
3. What can I *adapt (A)*?
4. How can I *modify (M)* or *magnify (M)*?
5. What can be *put to other uses (P)*?
6. What can be *eliminated (E)*?
7. What is a *reverse (R)* of this item or what *rearrangement (R)* can be made?

Commit the SCAMPER questions to memory and ask them repeatedly as you journey through problem-solving sessions.

Another offered by Michalko is called "Brainstorming Bulletin Board." It is useful with teams and groups as well as with larger units and is quite simple. A problem to be solved is placed in the center of the board. Post-it™ notes are available nearby. Interested parties are asked to suggest ideas, alternatives, and solutions, which they then stick on the board. I also use this technique with a cause-and-effect fishbone diagram in order to break down the problem into four major areas, such as people, policies, procedures, and materials.

## Maintenance

Much of this book has focused on the maintenance area, so I will not elaborate again. In summary, however, the group process consultant must have knowledge of and make decisions on assessment, type of intervention, level and intensity, and depth of intervention. He or she must be familiar with and recognize both overt and convert dynamics and act on them accordingly. Teams and groups cannot be fully successful without attention to maintenance. The maintenance dynamics provide the energy that drives the group.

## Conflict Management

One of the most feared and anxiety-producing maintenance areas in group work is managing conflict. Yet, the group members usually will not deal with conflict until the group process consultant models that behavior. That is, the consultant may have to draw fire towards himself or herself before participants will. Furthermore, the major difficulty exists *within* the group process consultant. While we may espouse conflict as good, desirable, and healthy, in actuality, we avoid and deny conflict, smooth it over, and implicitly work to suppress its eruption. If group process consultants are to be competent, they must find effective ways to understand and work through their own conflict fears. On the cognitive side there are many excellent sources on the subject, including Gray (1989), Crum (1987), Moore (1986), Brown (1983), Pneuman and Bruehl (1982), Robert (1982), Fisher and Ury (1981), Hart (1981), and Filley (1975).

There are experiential workshops conducted to help the participant examine his or her conflict through activities, simulations, personal history, and skill practice. Cognitive-focused seminars tend not to be as helpful, as they may get to the head but not the "gut."

## SELF-KNOWLEDGE

Perhaps the most powerful tool is the group process consultant himself or herself. How the consultant presents himself or herself can have a great impact on the group. Some consultants exhibit warmth; others, a sense of aloofness—technically efficient perhaps but without much rapport.

Humor can be a double-edged sword. A group process consultant who has a great sense of humor and loves to engage in repartee told me of a situation that backfired. Ordinarily this style works well for him in groups and is an asset. In this particular instance, however, he tried to use humor after the group had done rather poorly in a behavioral assessment. The comments were seen as a put down by some of the participants and were received with anger and hostility. His credibility, at least temporarily, was lost. He discussed the incident with the group and was able to rectify the situation. In another setting or with a different audience, his style and humor might have been well accepted.

I use a list of questions that help to understand what is happening *to me* and therefore what is happening to the group (Reddy, in press):

What am I feeling at the moment?
What physical sensations accompany this situation?
What images and metaphors come to mind?
What aspects of myself or my behaviors do I criticize?
What aspects and behaviors of group members do I criticize?
What atypical thought patterns are occurring?
What assumptions do I make about the group or its members?
What expectations do I have about the group or particular members?
Am I resistive to members' suggestions or feedback?
How do I react to criticism, and in what areas?
What are my "triggers," or anxiety arousers?
Do I inhibit or encourage self-disclosure in myself or in group members?
Where and what do I rationalize?
What do I dream about after a group session?

These questions (and you can create your own) help us use ourselves as assessment tools. Our intuition is very powerful if we give it a chance.

## Personal Development

"The most critical issue facing us, I believe, is that which surrounds *personal development* training, that is, of group specialists, leaders, trainers, counselors, and facilitators. While there are numerous programs aimed at training the group specialist, there seems to be a decreasing number of programs which focus *in depth* on the specialist as *the instrument of change.* There should be, I believe, a major focus and considerable self-work in self-awareness and personal development in order for one to become an *effective* practitioner" (Reddy, 1985, p. 106).

During the 1960s and early 1970s, it seemed that group practitioners more readily raised their personal and societal self-consciousness about issues. Personal behaviors, attitudes, and assumptions were examined. There were T-groups, sensitivity training, college seminars, encounter groups, Tavistock, and weekend marathons. The human potential movement flourished.

At present, a few training organizations, such as the NTL (National Training Laboratories) Institute and some universities continue to offer these human-interaction groups and workshops. Human-interaction groups remain a good beginning vehicle for self-exploration and interpersonal awareness. They offer a setting where the participant can probe his or her feelings and try new conflict-coping behaviors.

A *caveat:* These groups—like yours—are as good and as effective as the person conducting them. Not unlike group process consultants, there are competent and incompetent group facilitators, trainers, and consultants. These groups do not substitute for psychotherapy, nor were they so created. Unfortunately, some participants join groups for a "quick cure." Behavioral change does not occur without the pain of self-examination over an extended period of time and, usually, with the help of a professional.

## Values

What are the values we hold about working people? Our values are the windows through which we see our world. We see what we are, and our values are what we are. These values determine how we view the world of work and also the group participants with whom we work. If a practitioner's value is "working alone for self-aggrandizement," serving as a group process consultant will probably not reward him or her nor help the group.

Likewise, a value on directing and controlling is incompatible with group process consultation. The potential impact of values on our work obligates the group process consultant to clarify, understand, and explicate his or her values. Chapter Eight discusses values and ethics.

## Style

Style is one's idiosyncratic way of behaving. These consistent behavioral characteristics grow out of our values, attitudes, and preferences. Although one can learn to change behaviors, others are more entrenched and characterological. Some behaviors are counter to effective group work. Feedback from group participants is the most potent way to learn about what works and what does not work. Valid and standardized instruments are useful in understanding the nature of one's style.

## Giving and Receiving Feedback

Skill in giving feedback and receptivity to receiving feedback are critical for the group process consultant. The consultant cannot hope to foster these skills in the group if he or she cannot manage feedback. One can learn feedback skills by following guidelines for effective feedback (Jacobs, 1974; Seashore, Seashore, & Weinberg, 1991) and by frequently practicing these appropriate behaviors. The criteria for useful feedback require the giver to:

- Be descriptive rather than evaluative;
- Be specific rather than general;
- Offer feedback rather than impose;
- Give feedback at the earliest opportunity;
- Direct the feedback at behavior that can be changed;

- Consider the needs of the receiver as well as one's own;
- Check with the receiver to see if the message has been heard;
- Suggest that the receiver check out the feedback with others; and
- Leave the decision for change with the receiver.

The receiver is also required to:

- Listen;
- Not respond defensively;
- Paraphrase what he or she has heard;
- Try to capture the feelings of the sender;
- Consider what he or she has heard;
- Check out the data with others;
- Consider changing the behavior if it checks out;
- And, again, listen.

The fine feedback research conducted by the West Virginia group (Jacobs, 1974; Jacobs, Feldman, & Cavior, 1973; Jacobs, Jacobs, Gatz, & Schaible, 1973; Schaible & Jacobs, 1975) has been largely ignored by work groups and teams. Yet, their findings have dynamic implications in the work world. Their results show the following:

- Situations that provide for a greater exchange of feedback among small group participants than would take place spontaneously will lead to superior outcomes.
- Subjects rated positive feedback as more accurate than they rated negative feedback.
- Positive feedback was rated as more desirable, affecting subjects more than negative feedback, and promoting a greater intention to change.
- Negative *behavioral* feedback (i.e., that which describes the other person's behavior) was assessed as more cred-

ible than negative *emotional* feedback (i.e., that which describes one's own feelings).

- Positive *behavioral* feedback was rated as most credible and negative feedback as least credible under conditions of anonymous delivery.

- Positive and negative *emotional* feedback were not significantly different in credibility when the identity of the deliverer was not given.

- The delivery of positive feedback first will increase the probability of acceptance of negative feedback later in an intervention.

## Managing Diversity

We are moving toward a global economy and already experience the benefits of increased numbers of minorities and women in the U.S. work force. In addition, the U.S. population is getting older. The group process consultant is obliged to work issues, concerns, and conflicts around gender, race, age, differently abled—and all of the *isms*. The consultant must be prepared to deal with his or her own issues, assumptions, and biases in these areas.

## Strengths and Limitations

We all have strengths and limitations as consultants, managers, participants, and staff members. Performing a periodic audit of our strengths and limitations, with honest and constructive feedback from group members, superiors, peers, and colleagues—and family members—is a difficult but worthwhile venture. As group process consultants, as human beings, it is reasonable that we continue to grow and develop personally and professionally.

## Gender Differences

Are women better group process consultants than men? I believe generally, they are. Whether they are innately better, I do not know, nor do I know of empirical data to support my assertion. There are anecdotal data (Tannen, 1990), however. Female group process consultants, in general, seem more attuned to group needs and to members' needs. Perhaps most important, female consultants approach problem solving less competitively than men and more collaboratively. In summary, women consultants tend to model the process approach itself.

Conversely, I also see women who are rigidly socialized into the male work model. Their approach is directive, technique oriented, competitive, and minimally collaborative. This is an area in which empirical research is needed.

---

### Intervention Consideration

*Group-on-Group.* There are times when the group process consultant may wish to accent differences in the group (e.g., talkers/nontalkers or men/women). The consultant suggests that each group take a turn at being observed by the other group. After twenty minutes, the outer group shares its observations or comments on the dynamics of the inner group. This can be done publicly or in pairs of inner-outer circle participants. A caution, however: This intervention can surface competition between subgroups, which then must be worked out.

---

## The Role of Intuition

Beyond the learned competencies, some group process consultants are simply better than others. The group process consultant must use intuition to be highly effective. Intuition has to do with that "gut" feeling, making connections, "hunches," and what is "going on" at many different levels. There is some empirical evidence that supports this contention. Bushe and Gibbs (1990) found that intuition ("N" as measured by the Myers-Briggs Type Indicator) and the stage of ego development predicted consulting competence as rated by the subjects' peers and trainers. When the two measures were entered into a structural equation, ego development remained as the positive predictor.

Hamilton (1988), in a multivariate analysis, also found evidence that intuition, as measured by the Myers-Briggs Type Indicator, strongly and significantly related to consultant effectiveness: "Sensing was negatively related and intuition positively related to effectiveness" (p. 53). Sensing people are more immediate and tend to work within what is specific and concretely known. Intuitive people make decisions based on "hunches," have tolerance for ambiguity, and tend to see relationships and meaning beyond the immediate.

## THE DEVELOPMENTAL PLAN

I recommend the creation of a detailed developmental plan that permits consultants to envision their practice three to five years into the future. The plan moves from broad philosophical strokes to specific action plans. Where do you see yourself in group process consultation in the next three to five years? Imagine that you are on a magic carpet. You have the ability to look down at yourself in your role as group process consultant. Let your imagination soar. What are you doing? What do you look like when you are at your best? What behaviors are you exhibiting? This flight into fantasy can be quite helpful in creating your plan. Be spontaneous, idealistic, and specific.

Now, write out the scenario. What were the values driving this vision? What values do you want to drive it? Achievement? Excitement? Innovation? Remuneration? What are your wants and desires? They may be as simple as conducting one group a year in process consultation to becoming a major portion of your practice, internal or external. What are your needs in this area? Training in process consultation might be enough to make you a better facilitator, or you may need basic and advanced training to enhance your capability as a serious group process consultant.

Once you have your values, vision, and needs articulated, it is time to become specific. How are you going to attain this vision? First of all, what is your covenant? To what are you willing to commit yourself? It might range from group process consultation as a piece of your practice to the best group process consultant in town— or the country. Now set your goal. Specifically, concretely, detailed, what are your goals for each of the next three years? Include position, money, amount of work, whatever you can commit to lead you to your vision. Next comes the *how*. How are you going to attain these goals? In essence, what do you need to do? This will involve specific steps, such as "I need to have my manager approve my working with three groups in the next quarter."

You will probably have a number of these steps. Finally, you will need even smaller steps or tactics to get you there. Using the previous example, add, "I will meet with my manager on Monday, at 2:00 p.m., to discuss the matter and lay out my plan" or "I know managers who could use my help. I'll contact each on Tuesday and offer my services." The key is *detailed* planning. Locke and Latham (1984, 1990) extol the value of goal setting and offer sound rationale, evidence, and support for the approach.

Group process consultation is deceiving. From the outside it looks easy; "anyone can do it." Dealing with human behavior at best is difficult. Working with groups—while the group is working—is particularly difficult. It requires education, training, feedback, and experience. Beyond this, group process consultation is also an art that requires self-knowledge and the use of intuition.

Chapter Eight explores the values and ethics of the group process consultant and how the process can be embedded into the life of the organization.

## Executive Planning Team ♦ ♦ ♦

During subsequent meetings, the team continued to struggle with the problem of lack of collaboration. Data generating was excellent, as was a host of ideas for solutions. When it came to selecting one or two or combining related solutions, the group fell short. A few managers were reluctant to give up ownership of their ideas or have them "contaminated" by merging them. When Scott pointed this out via a behavior description, it did little good.

Scott then suggested a group-on-group configuration. He split the group in half; while one half worked, the other half observed the process and made notes. Each person in the center had been paired with an observer. The inside group worked for a half-hour and then was given feedback by the outside partners. The process was reversed for the second thirty minutes. A general discussion then took place regarding the process and dynamics.

What Scott had commented on previously emerged from the group. This time team members took ownership for their lack of collaboration. Scott suggested it might have to do with competition among members. This comment opened a storm of discussion about personal competition within the group and in the workplace in general. Sam acknowledged his feelings of competition. Jerry pointed out that competition between managers was reinforced in the organizational culture. After much discussion the group adjourned. The atmosphere at the next meeting was strikingly different. Although the intensity was still there, there were clear attempts at collaboration. Scott pointed out these attempts and asked members how they felt about them and the impact on the task. There was general agreement that the group had "turned the corner," as Sam put it.

## Quality Circles ♦ ♦ ♦

*Circle I.* The previous session was a breakthrough for Circle I. Although somewhat anxiety arousing for members to deal with their conflicts and competition, it showed conflict could be addressed constructively. With the issues now manageable, the circle had renewed interest and motivation. Within a month Circle I presented three proposals to management. One of the proposals was challenged, but the group, with Kim's help, had anticipated the questions. They had role played a number of scenarios and were well prepared. Two recommendations were put into effect immediately. The challenged proposal was accepted with modifications and sent "upstairs." The group was pleased with their work and accomplishments.

*Circle II.* The creative problem-solving techniques brought about unexpected benefits for Circle II. The new methodology and techniques permitted the group to experiment with more creative approaches and solutions. This, in turn, generated more interaction and conflict. Although the group had reached a level of conflict management with which they were comfortable, they were now confronted with staying at that level or moving beyond it.

Michael suggested they request a trainer from the ·human resources department to conduct a conflict-management workshop. The trainer came in for a full day with a program tailored around the specific needs of the group. Circle II worked as hard on their conflict-management skills as they had with creative problem solving. They took on a variety of increasingly complex problems and dealt with most at a high level of commitment and ingenuity.

*Circle III.* At the end of two months, Circle III had developed two proposals. On presentation, they were challenged by management for their incompleteness but taken under advisement. Larry did not set another meeting with the group to discuss their reactions or next steps. The group did not meet again, nor were their proposals acted on.

## Hospital Administration ♦ ♦ ♦

The next session showed a striking change in the atmosphere of the group. Lucia was energetic but not frenetic nor hostile. Jeremy was both open and task oriented. Other members now with renewed energy were ready to work on task. Laura suggested they recontract with one another around a new set of behavioral norms. This they did and discussed working on task through an agenda. If they had problems they agreed to stop and work with Laura on maintenance issues. Indeed, this occurred on several occasions as Lucia drifted into old behavior. However, members confronted her immediately and the situations were worked through. In addition, members challenged one another, at first cautiously, and then more assertively. A good balance of task and maintenance behaviors was established, and Laura allowed the group members to manage their own process.

# Group Process Consultation and the Organization

# 8

*T*his chapter explores two major, yet neglected, areas in group process consultation:

1. Values and ethics, and

2. Embedding group process consultation into the fabric of the organization.

These two areas are included together because they are mediated, if not determined, by the macro-organizational culture. Does the culture support the values of process consultation? Will group process consultation be accepted as a legitimate area of intervention or as a luxury to be used sparingly and only with high level groups?

## VALUE AND ETHICAL CONSIDERATIONS

There are no legislative nor formal ethics and values to which the group process consultant must adhere. However, in related fields, similar thought and work has been done that can and should be applied to group process consultation.

Gellermann (1985) differentiates *values* and *ethics*. Values "refers to those qualities or things (such as behaviors, results, beliefs, and attitudes) that are considered desirable, important, or worthy" (p. 396). Ethics "refers to standards of judgment and conduct" (p. 396). Gellermann maintains that values, given they are more fundamental, are the foundation for ethics, a position with which I agree. We will use this distinction in this chapter to examine the values and ethics of the group process consultant.

## VALUES

Certainly not all group process consultants will agree with my choice of values. However, these values represent the bias of many group process consultants in the field.

## Spirit of Inquiry

Bennis (1966) describes the spirit of inquiry as the value position of science that includes thinking about, investigating, and experimenting with problems. It is "a love of truth relentlessly pursued" (p. 48). Applied, it suggests that anything and everything is "grist-for-the-mill" as it relates to the effective and efficient functioning and creativity of the group.

In the education piece and in the contract, the group process consultant explains this value as "Everything is relevant for discussion inasmuch as it relates to task accomplishment."

## Collaboration

A fundamental value in group work is collaboration. The group process consultant and the group members enter into a mutual contract to reach articulated goals and objectives. The group is the client. The group process consultant does not enter into subcontracts, explicit or implicit, with other members, manager, or administration.

For example, a group process consultant focuses on covert conflict between two members. One responds, indicating he will talk to the second member after the group adjourns. Group process consultant: "As we discussed before I came into the group and in formulating the contract, whatever happens in here affects the entire group. There is value in openly talking about your conflict. I suspect it will be helpful to both of you, and perhaps there are other members who relate to it or at least can give their perspective on it."

## Respect for the Rights of Group Members

Group members work for and are paid by the organization. This does not mean, however, that the consultant should disregard situations when group members are coerced, manipulated, and treated with disrespect by the organization. Consultants collude with management when they ignore such behaviors and attitudes, obvious or subtle. An example is when the group process consultant accepts an assignment while realizing from the start it will fail because of the larger organizational culture or reward system. Currently, self-directed teams are springing up throughout the country. In many organizations neither the climate nor the reward system is conducive to such teams. Consultants are aware of the situation, but some will help initiate the effort without considering the larger systemic issues.

## Personal Satisfaction in Work

Work satisfaction and the fulfillment of appropriate personal needs in the work setting are legitimate goals. They are not counter to productivity nor to goal attainment. Although contented workers are not necessarily more productive, work satisfaction obliges the group process consultant to intervene, when appropriate, in this area.

This value also encourages the use of maintenance interventions. That is, it is legitimate to raise questions about a group member's feelings as it relates to task. The intervention may not necessarily change the situation, but it is a statement that a group member's well-being and self-esteem are important and relevant.

## High Performance

The vision and quest for a high-performing group or team require interventions by the consultant that a lesser performance would not demand. Should every group be high performing? Probably not, but each group should have an opportunity to decide that question with the help of the consultant. The consultant must make the question explicit if it is his or her value.

A group process consultant described the characteristics and demands of a high-performing team to a cluster of three teams in the education phase. It was emphasized by the consultant that there was no onus in not moving toward high performance if the reasons were discussed and understood. The groups spent considerable time assessing their own characteristics, dynamics, and relevance to the company. One team, of the three, felt it should and could be high performing. The other two, for a variety of reasons, believed they would be better served by setting a different standard of performance and still contributing to the company effort. It was a prudent decision and one that reduced greatly unnecessary stress and expectations.

## Respect for the Sponsor

The *sponsor* in this context is the person(s) or group charging the client with its task and who will pass or sign off on the final product. This typically is the organization and its management. I have seen group process consultants empower a group to "do their own thing," with total disregard for the sponsor. Of course, it was the group members who suffered when the objectives were not reached to the sponsor's satisfaction.

In one case the group in question had to deliver its report in a scant four weeks. Instead of reducing process loss by keeping the group focused, on track, and task oriented, the consultant continually pushed the maintenance issues to the exclusion of the task. Not only were the maintenance issues not managed, they engendered more conflict. The end result, as one might expect, was that the delivery date came without a product. The consultant defended his interventions by saying the group was not capable of dealing with their issues.

## Group Member Competence

The group process consultant values the capability of group members to learn the fundamentals of processing and reinforces those behaviors. We learned to be consultants. In time, with intervention practice and reinforcement, so, too, can group members learn to process themselves. Equally, members should not be expected to become consultants nor to make interventions in areas in which they are not trained.

As the maxim goes, "Trust the process." In time, and with patience and affirmation, group members will manage much of their own process. If they do not go as deeply as the consultant would like, it may well be they have reached their appropriate level. To be pushed further could be dysfunctional.

## Honesty

We value and foster appropriate honesty and disclosure in the group setting. This is determined by contract, type of group, objectives, stage of group development, and the norms set by the group. Promoting *total* honesty can be inappropriate, disruptive, and counterproductive.

In one of the early sessions of a mixed gender, race, and management-level group the external group process consultant insisted on members' impressions of one another. Members complied. The results were devastating. Members felt hurt, abused, put-down. The consultant had not conducted an adequate assessment, nor did he have a contract with the group. When the group met again, it was with a new, internal, consultant who, fortunately, was able to do excellent *damage control*.

## Balance of Task and Maintenance Process

An interactive group oriented exclusively toward task or maintenance will probably not be effective nor create a high-quality product. While a balance is optimal, maintenance is in the service of the task. The challenge to the group process consultant is to stretch the group to its capability. Maintenance interventions must be made to deal with the issues at hand and at a level the group can manage at the moment and permit it to move on task.

## Responsibility for Behavior

The group members and the group process consultant are responsible for their own behaviors. There is a greater ethical responsibility for the consultant because of his or her unique role, perceived authority, and potential influence on the group members.

Group process consultants sometimes forget they are group members *but in a different role*. They are responsible for modeling behavior and for reminding members, when necessary, that not all behaviors are permissible. Boundary management is important for both consultant and other members.

## Group Versus Individual Needs

I have spoken of the group members and the legitimacy of fulfilling personal needs. The group, too, has needs. At times the needs of individuals are in conflict with the needs of the group. This situation is most obvious when members insist on having their own way. It is also manifest in group process consultants who insist on maintenance not in the service of task. The appurtenant needs of the group must take precedence over the individual's and the group process consultant's needs.

## Risk Taking

Creative and quality decisions require risk taking by members. To move the group to its boundaries demands risk taking by the group process consultant. The group members should not be pushed too fast nor too soon. They need to know and agree, via the contract, that the consultant will foster and encourage risk taking in the forms of disclosure, challenge, emotional expression, creative problem solving, and dealing with conflict.

A technique that can foster appropriate risk taking is to suggest group members pair off (sometimes called support dyads) after each meeting for just fifteen minutes. Dyad membership is permanent. Their focus is to give feedback to each other as to how effective they were in the group today, how much risk they took to help the group move forward, and what they plan to do the next time. This skill-focused technique has proven to be very effective.

## Conflict

Conflict around substantive issues and content is valued, as is the management of interpersonal conflict. Conflict is healthy, natural, and desirable. It is encouraged by the group process consultant as a way of generating different ideas and pathways and eventually creative solutions. It is often necessary to ask, "Is everyone in the group *really* in favor of this idea?"

A way for encouraging conflict is the *devil's-advocate* technique. Before a final decision is made or an action plan implemented or at other appropriate junctures, two or three group members are assigned devil's-advocate roles. Their focus is to challenge, push, attempt to shoot down, and discredit what is proposed. The arguments are to be issue focused (*ad rem*) and not *ad hominem.* The discussions will be heated and intense but legitimized and accepted. They will also lead to members' understanding, experientially, the value of conflict.

## Diversity

As discussed above, diversity in gender, race, ethnicity, and age brings a richness from which new ideas and solutions can emerge. We have fostered mediocrity in the United States because of an exclusive homogeneous white-male approach to problem solving and decision making. With the changing work population this homogeneity is diluted. The organizational work groups of the next century will look very different from those at present, but we must give members the skill training necessary for effective group membership.

## ETHICS

As in any helping profession, the moral and ethical considerations in group process consultation are basic yet often subtle.

## Basic Considerations

First, the process consultant has a primary responsibility to protect all group members. This does not mean that members should be prevented from confronting one another. Indeed, conflict is fostered for creative problem solving. It does mean that group members should not be singled out in such a way that they are scapegoated. When a consultant has a group "problem person," it is quite easy to collude in setting up that member to be inappropriately focused on by other group members.

The task and maintenance work of the group must be done within the group setting. A common practice among consultants and facilitators is to take issues off line. This practice is often under the guise of not wanting to disturb the work of the group. More likely, it relates to the inability or reluctance of the consultant to deal with conflict within the group. Taking issues, problems, and the people involved off line is to dilute important group energy. It promotes distrust of the consultant and precludes the development of group cohesion.

Determining who is the client is not usually seen as an ethical issue. However, it does dictate with whom the consultant shares information and perceptions of the group's dynamics. If the process consultant determines that the entire group is the client—and 90 percent of the time this should be the case—then it would be unethical for the process consultant to discuss the group, its members, and the dynamics with anyone but the group *as a whole*. Quite often, the consultant is influenced by the power and authority of the manager or executive and will discuss group progress to a point of giving detailed information. Curiously, if a group member tried to discuss dynamics with the consultant, the consultant would probably refuse and even chastise the group member for raising issues outside the group.

## Monetary Issues

A major ethical issue, dilemma perhaps, is around the general question of process consultation. Facilitating and conducting training and organization development do not guarantee expertise in micro process consultation. I have been called into several major organizations for damage control after a trainer or facilitator had inappropriately served as group process consultant. In most of these cases, the "consultants" (1) had little knowledge of group dynamics and (2) were not trained nor skilled in making maintenance process interventions. There is a tendency for some consultants, once they have made organizational entry, to see themselves as all things to all people. This is fine when they have had the training and experience to back it up, but frequently the driving factor is monetary.

A final ethical issue considered here is consultant fees. It is a topic discussed among consultants but rarely written about. One would like to think consultants' fees are based on some criteria and rationale. Certainly the consultant's training, experience, track record, referrals, and referral sources should come into consideration—with a recognition that there are "going rates" and the principle of supply and demand.

There are far too many consultants who consider the latter two dimensions and ignore the first set. For example, in one client system, consultants agreed among themselves what fees to charge the client system. The client, not having experience nor expertise, thought process consultants were required in each group, two or three times a week. The consultants recognized, given the tasks of the group, one or one-and-a-half days of work would be sufficient. Instead the consultants colluded and charged the client system an unconscionable amount of money. It certainly was not in the best interest of the client system. The consultants rationalized the process by saying it was what the client wanted: "We were responding to the client's wishes; if we didn't do it, someone else would." Often, ethical issues seem to be relevant for the other consultant but not to oneself.

What are the standards and judgments of good conduct in group process consultation? There are many, of course, but the group process consultant should be aware of and sensitive to the most fundamental.

## Self-Knowledge

The first ethical principle is knowledge of oneself. That is, the group process consultant is obligated to examine his or her beliefs, assumptions, and values. He or she must also struggle with issues of racism, gender, and especially those that generate conflict.

In addition, consultants must learn the boundaries and limitations of their competence. This knowledge requires education, training, and supervision with feedback.

## Contracts and Agreements

A clear and explicit contract in collaboration with the client will minimize future difficulties. Written agreements are preferred to oral, and oral to none. The information includes understandings, expectations, time lines, roles, and evaluation.

## Access to Information

Group members should have access to whatever information the consultant has generated through instruments, surveys, and interviews. It should be handled anonymously but not confidentially. Rarely are there surprises about information. Group members know the issues and problems. They have been talking about them for extended periods of time, usually behind closed doors or in the rest rooms. While names and identities may have to be protected, summarized and group data should be shared for the group to understand its dynamics.

One of the advantages of building in an education phase to the flow of group process consultation is the occasion to inform the client of these conditions.

## Disclosure

The diametrical side to access is protection of information, about the group and its members. As often stated in this book, the group is the client. Information is not taken off line nor shared with anyone without the *explicit* agreement of group members.

## Issues with Group Members

The group process consultant is responsible for his or her own behaviors, assumptions, and attributions. If the consultant has conflict and issues with a member, then it should be surfaced in the group. It must be done appropriately and with tact. Leaving covert such matters is unfair to the group member and may preclude the consultant's working optimally. It is also counter to the feedback model espoused for group effectiveness.

## Asking Why

Group process consultants should explicate their objectives and rationales. Group members should have an opportunity—at any time—to ask why an activity, exercise, or intervention has been performed. Satisfactory answers to questions promote psychological safety, foster trust, and increase consultant credibility.

## Accountability and Responsibility

The group process consultant is responsible for the psychological welfare of group members and the agreed-on interests of the sponsoring organization. If a consultant's values are inconsistent with the organization, he or she should decline the job. His or her role is not to subvert the organization, promote rebellion, or advocate sabotage. Although this situation may sound extreme, I have known of consultants who advocated behaviors *designed* to bring group members into high conflict with company hierarchy on the pretext that it would help change an oppressive culture. The consequences, of course, were disastrous.

In one case, group members, after working on difficult gender issues, experienced feelings of success and euphoria—the latter, in part, as a reduction in anxiety. However, in this "high," some members decided to directly challenge what they perceived as unfair organizational practices. The group consultants did not question the wisdom nor the potential implications of the proposed actions.

Predictably, management was angry, defensive, 'and ready to punish. Fortuitously, an organization development consultant, working with management, challenged the senior group to closely examine the situation *and their own behavior.* They did so, and as a result the employees were only mildly reprimanded, but the consultants' contract was terminated. It is not to say that changes were not needed in the organization; indeed, they were. However, the driving force was the consultants and in a setting where no systemic structures were yet in place for challenges and changes.

## Protection from Self and Others

Group members should also be protected from themselves (in the case of extreme self-deprecation) and from one another (in the case of scapegoating).

In one case, a group member made self-references whenever she spoke in the group, always ending with a description of how worthless she was. Other members were obviously uncomfortable, yet became irritated as she increasingly occupied group time. It developed into an atypical circumstance in which the group process consultant felt it necessary to meet with the member off line. With the help of the group process consultant and the support of her immediate supervisor, the member was counseled out of the group. The group process consultant wisely obtained permission from her to discuss briefly the situation with the group. This intervention permitted group members to discuss their own anxiety, fears, and guilt about her leaving.

In extreme and overt behaviors, scapegoating is not common. In more covert forms, however, scapegoating is a frequent occurrence. Picture the young manager who tried to find his place in a hastily created cross-functional group. He was outspoken and, unfortunately, often off target with his ideas, perceptions, and offerings. He became the butt of jokes and frequent negative comments and, over time, took on the tacit role of group buffoon. The situation became extreme, pervasive, and symptomatic of other covert behaviors. The functioning of the group was seriously compromised. The group was unable—or unwilling—to examine their behaviors or dynamics. Finally, the consultant recommended the group disband and reorganize with new members. The situation was delicately and well handled by the group process consultant, who accepted the idea that the group would not address the issues yet should not be positioned to be punished by management.

## Evaluation

How does the consultant know he or she is successful? Some form of evaluation, mutually agreed on by consultant and client, should be determined. This can range from joint discussion to instrumentation to objective criteria and observation. What is important is a joint discussion of expectations and how to determine group objectives, task and maintenance.

## Role Boundaries

Group process consultants often work with other professionals, managers, facilitators, and team leaders. The consultant must know his or her boundaries and be willing to raise issues of role conflict and role ambiguity. The consultant must discern when to say no. This could involve a project, job, a request from a manager, or a demand from the group.

Now that we have examined values and ethics, we turn to ways of establishing group process consultation in the organization.

## EMBEDDING GROUP PROCESS CONSULTATION IN THE ORGANIZATION

Before looking at specific ways of embedding group process consultation in the organization, we will explore some related dynamics and issues particular to the HRD (human resource development) and OD (organization development) roles. It is in these fields we find most group process consultants.

Many times the HRD consultant suggests group process consultation to a manager who responds with "group *what*?" Managers know some HRD and OD nomenclature, concepts, and jargon, but, for the most part, are unknowledgeable about what consultants actually know, do, and deliver. This ignorance can be blamed on HRD personnel, for we fail to educate organizations, executives, and managers about our areas of expertise and deliverables. "What can we do?" asks the HRD manager; "Usually, a VP or manager calls us and tells us what they want." That statement is probably accurate. But we fail at that entry point to respond to the manager and explore the boundaries of the problem or say, "No, I don't think that approach is in your best interest at this time." Instead, the typical scenario shows the HRD manager or representative accepting whatever job, problem, and issue that comes to the department.

HRD personnel fall into the trap of being an "expert" or "doctor," rather than acting consultatively. The expert model is the opposite of what we want in the organization. The international work culture is slowly becoming more participative, more group and team oriented. Organizational members will contribute to problem solving and decision making. Of course, there are the technical problems that require the expert, and that is appropriate; but most nontechnical problems, and some technical, require a consultative approach.

HRD personnel must, therefore, learn how to consult. This will take educating managers on how the consultant can be most helpful and how they—the managers—can, in turn, be more effective. Ralph H. Kilmann (1984, p.159)[2] offers twelve rules for problem management that should be put in the kit of all HRD personnel:

## Twelve Rules for Problem Management

1. Plan before doing; don't attack a complex problem blindly and foolishly.

2. Subdivide a complex problem into parts; don't lose sight of the forest because of all the trees.

3. Make assumptions explicit; don't let quicksand be the foundation for your arguments.

---

[2] From *Beyond the Quick Fix: Managing Five Tracks to Organizational Success* by Ralph H. Kilmann. San Francisco: Jossey-Bass Inc., Publishers, 1984. Used with permission of the publisher.

4. Test assumptions; don't assume that everyone sees the problem your way.

5. Debate assumptions and positions before any consensus is reached; don't be afraid of productive conflict.

6. Define the problem before solving it; don't implement a quick fit to the wrong problem.

7. Collaborate on complex problems; don't stifle any available information—it may come back to haunt you.

8. Look to the deviant when the problem is complex; don't assume the majority is correct—it had common ignorance.

9. Foster trust and candor in gathering information; don't develop a CYA atmosphere.

10. Consult/join on complex, important problems; don't force your simple solution on others, expecting them to accept it.

11. Tell/sell on simple, unimportant problems; don't bother others—they have more important things to do.

12. Stop and examine the problem management process at every meeting; don't assume it takes care of itself—it doesn't.

How can this be accomplished? If internal HRD and OD organizations had to survive as do external consultants, they would more readily consider a range of strategies for professionalism, marketing, and profitability.

## Learn to Say No

Perhaps because of organizational culture, the evolved role of HRD and OD, or personality, the change agents seem to respond to every whim and request of management—even when it is not in the manager's best interest. This approach is clearly not in the *consultant's* best interest. When something does go wrong, the consultant often bears the blame. We need to learn to say *no* by presenting a rationale and offering an alternative approach.

## Take a Consultative Approach

I have heard consultants say, "I knew this was going to be a disaster, but what could I do?" What the consultant might have done was say *no* to the manager and then consult with him or her—discussing problem description, assumptions, feelings, alternative strategies, and finally tentative action steps.

## Professional Presentation of Self

By saying *no*, when appropriate, and taking a consultative approach, you act and are seen as helpful. The approach is to help the client explore alternatives after clearly defining the problem and gathering valid data. Managers, of course, need to be educated about a consultative approach. Typically, they have been trained—and rewarded—for quick, "expert" answers and results. The days of the *heroic* manager (Bradford & Cohen, 1984) are numbered. The information era is fast, vast, and complex. It will requires *all* of us to assess, problem solve, and decide (Weisbord, 1987). To present oneself as helpful in this culture is to present oneself as a competent professional who knows what he or she is capable of. It means resisting the temptation to say, "I can do that," when one cannot do that and knows full well that the manager will also need help in his or her quest.

To embed group process consultation into the organization, the internal consultant must start by first thinking of his or her unit as a profit center or as an external consulting firm: "What do we have to do to survive? What strategies must we have in place to turn a profit?" The following suggestions may help internal consultants answer these questions.

## Let People Know What Your Unit Delivers

HRD consultants tend to assume that managers know and understand what consultants do and have to offer. Discussions with managers reveals the opposite. They think of HRD personnel when they cannot resolve a conflict or manage a problem. Managers tend to be crisis oriented and not prevention educated. HRD consultants must raise the awareness of the manager about human resources services, including group process consultation. This can be done in a number of ways limited only by the HRD unit's creativity and inventiveness.

It helps when the human resources staff members have pride in their unit and in their services. Pride certainly seems to enhance professionalism.

## Meetings With Managers

It is unfortunate that consultants do not meet with managers until there is a crisis, issue, or a request. Under these conditions it is more difficult to become acquainted and to explore services and options. Consultants should *make* the time before the crisis to meet with managers. Arrange individual or small group meetings to talk about the services you and your unit provide and the conditions under which they can best be provided. Elicit what expectations managers have regarding consultation.

## Make Cold Calls

Spend time on the floor. Conduct JIT (just-in-time) consultation. We recommend this practice to managers and executives; why not to the HRD person? Make "cold" (unannounced) calls. If the manager is busy, the consultant should not intrude upon his or her time. However, consultants are often surprised to find that a manager is happy to take a break, socialize for a short time, and find out what HRD or OD can do for him or her.

## Conduct Demos

Bringing together small groups of managers, executives, and other key and appropriate people to demonstrate the nature, content, and examples of group process consultation can be very powerful. One human resources unit did, in essence, a role play for regularly scheduled groups of managers to illustrate to usefulness of process consultation. Later, the HR staff members arranged to meet with each manager to discuss how they might initiate group process consultation in their team-oriented organization. During the demos, opportunity can be given managers to raise particular problems they would like to see worked through. A scenario is set and then the "actors" role play how their particular situation might be dealt with. Invariably, the manager gains insight into the situation and learns how he or she can better manage the situation. If the actual manager can be brought into the role play, all the better.

Conducting demo sessions can take up as little as one hour. It also gives managers an opportunity to share mutual problems.

## Videos

If managers simply cannot or choose not to take the time for a demo, either a real-play or role-play video can be used. Of course, if an actual case is used, permission must be obtained from all participants. However, in most organizations this is rarely a problem.

The video need not be lengthy. The primary objective is to give the viewer a sense of what group process consultation is. Thus, it must contain examples of task-process and maintenance-process interventions. It is helpful to give a four- to ten-minute input on the flow of process consultation and an explanation of content and process. Managers are urged to view the video when they have the opportunity.

## Electronic Mail

*E-mail* is now in most major organizations, both for-profit and not-for-profit. Although the systems may be already glutted with trivia and not-so-relevant information, the medium offers another avenue for contact with large numbers of people. A monthly item of interest or a brief description of HRD services can be very effective.

## Brochures

The human resources unit, like the external consultant firm, needs constantly to keep its name and the names of its members in the eye of the organization. Group process consultants can write memoranda or create newsletters explaining what they do.

Independent consultants find it valuable to describe their organization and services in copy for public examination. A well-thought-out and nicely designed brochure can be highly effective. Few organizations produce such copy, yet managers report the value of having such brochures to which they can refer. The copy needs to be professionally produced.

## Newsletters

Monthly or quarterly newsletters from the human services department describe activities, list services, and explore specific organizational issues. Newsletters keep the name and function of human resources in highlights. They also educate the potential client. Comments by a "guest" manager foster the perception that HRD is an integral part of the organization. The newsletters need to be created and produced professionally. This is hardly a problem with the present-day state of desk-top publishing.

## Selected Monthly Articles

A great deal of interesting and valuable information comes across the desk of the HRD staff. Selecting and sending to managers and executives topical issues, relevant articles, and simply interesting items help to educate and to change the norms of the organization. One should not overwhelm them with four or five articles; one brief relevant piece monthly is sufficient. The HRD staff also often has a variety of books available for managers, should they wish to read them.

If the human resources or consulting unit of the company wishes to be seen as credible, competent, and professional, it is imperative for that unit to take a proactive stance. Let's face it, when "downsizing," "right sizing," and "employee-number adjustment" are the words of the day, the HRD unit is the first to go. We in the human resources business have colluded in that process by not presenting ourselves as competent and professional as we might. Too often we have not actively reached out to the organization. Instead, we have been content to let the organization come to us, and then we have attempted to comply with anything it wished. Those human resource organizations and practitioners that remain reactive will not survive to the turn of the century.

## Educate, Educate, Educate

The process consultation area is, without doubt, exciting and rewarding. One can see and experience immediately the impact of his or her interventions. However, the work of the process consultant is difficult at best. Group members ignore or resist interventions or comply without exploring them. Participants want "how to's" and specific direction from the "expert" and often will not take responsibility for their own learning. Of course, if the consultant attempts to be "expert," this is also rejected.

In most businesses, employees work in task-and-results cultures with little regard for "feelings." Indeed, the word itself may be anathema. Processing may be cynically decried as "touchy-feely," or as that "sensitivity [expletive]." Moreover, we are so task driven and results oriented that a Herculean effort is required to get a group to become *problem oriented*. Getting the job done means to many content only or a total task process—but certainly not maintenance.

Regardless of how well prepared the group, feedback—particularly negative feedback—is usually received with a jolt. People do not like to be disconfirmed, regardless of how well delivered the feedback. Defensiveness and resistance rise quickly and are not easily quelled or removed.

Working through issues takes time, as does the acquisition of skills required to do so. Because of our "do-it-now" mentality, or as it has been described, "...wanting to get there before you arrive," employees in general and managers in particular do not want to spend the time on processing. We must find ways of showing them it is worth the time—and that it is cost effective.

The HRD member must begin to think *education*. Every opportunity to illustrate the value of consultation must be used. Not only will it enhance your work, it may well save your job. We know that lasting change comes about with cognitive and experiential learning, practice, and time. We must first raise the awareness that change is needed, then explain the nature of that change and how we can contribute to managing the change. Only well-planned education of our clients will move us toward our goal.

Chapter Nine—the final chapter—looks at a wide range of conditions, variables, and interventions that relate to group process consultation.

## Executive Planning Team ♦ ♦ ♦

The team was able to focus well on its planning and, after a few months, was comfortable in breaking into subgroups to work on tasks. While members joked about "trust," it clearly was there.

At times they would become too "tasky" and ignore their maintenance issues, but Scott—or some team member—would bring them back. Likewise, they would periodically become too engrossed in their own maintenance and let the task slide. Over time they did more and more of their own processing, kidding Scott about his "uselessness." Scott was sensitive to this but checked it out, however. It was important than he not lose his effectiveness, which was not the case.

The final major group issue was *insularity*. As the group continued its work and became increasingly cohesive, it began to ignore input and feedback from the outside. When Scott pointed this out, team members reacted angrily. The anger was disproportionate to the comment. Rather than push the issue, Scott opted to wait them out.

They worked on task for another forty-five minutes, when Jerry commented, "You know, maybe we could use some fresh ideas in here."

Bill added, "Geez, I don't want Scott to think he was right again."

Everyone, including Scott, laughed. A fruitful discussion followed on group and task needs. Arrangements were made to bring in resource people. Team members themselves designed the format and used a variety of activities as Scott had used with them, such as observers, empty chair, and so on. Care was taken to explain to resource people how they would be used and why.

## Quality Circles ♦ ♦ ♦

*Circle I.* Members asked Kim what they might learn to be more effective. Kim suggested their continued processing and perhaps additional training in creative problem-solving methods. Kim asked if they would like to work on more complex problems. They were unanimous in the affirmative response. Arrangements were made for group training in creative problem-solving methods. Landau volunteered to speak to their sponsor about introducing more complex problems. The sponsor was both surprised and elated. He had not quite expected this level of success with any circle. He was happy to comply but was astute enough to increase the complexity within manageable boundaries. He discussed the problem and his thinking with the circle, who appreciated his honesty and faith in them.

*Circle II.* Michael had loosened up over the year and a half as leader of Circle II. As his confidence grew as its leader, he was described as "not as standoffish or intellectual as you were." However, Michael felt he had gone about as far as could in changing his behavior. His reputation had grown in the company, as had Kim's in Circle I.

## Hospital Administration ◆ ◆ ◆

A series of crises hit the group as they were forced to confront difficult choices about the future of the hospital. Group members talked with and interviewed many hospital personnel, consumers, physicians, and town administrators. The data, although complete, tended to overload the executive committee. They were able, however, to share their concerns, anxieties, frustrations, and fears. This was a radical change from six months ago. Their venting led to a discussion around getting help and creating a number of committees to help with the planning. Each member of the executive committee would hold membership on one the ad hoc committees.

The plan exceeded their expectations. Hospital personnel were excited about being part of the change process in a very real way. Each committee had a facilitator from HRD and was trained in a four-day crash course. Committees met, people were interviewed, plans were drawn up and discussed, battles were fought, conflict was managed, and excitement was pervasive.

# Potpourri

# 9

*This* chapter includes a discussion of a range of miscellaneous roles, interventions, and questions and answers about groups and group process consultation that do not neatly fit into other chapters.

## GROUP PROCESS CONSULTATION STEREOTYPES

Like most group roles, the behaviors of group process consultants can become quite hackneyed. The following examples illustrate a range of stereotypical consultant and facilitator roles too often found in the group setting. These roles are also taken by members who do not perceive themselves as such, but our focus here is on the group process consultant and his or her role. The descriptions here are in caricature to illustrate the roles more clearly.

## Director

The Director overtly and covertly instructs the group on what to do and when to do it. This may be through maintenance as well as through task interventions. It is most commonly seen in group process consultants who have been around for a while. They have seen it all; they do not like the slow speed of the group and believe they can get the group to its destination faster than anyone else. The result may be compliance but not much real learning nor later transfer of skills.

| **Dr. Feelgood** | "Everything is just fine; there's no reason to get excited about all of this." This group process consultant is consistent with Blake and Mouton's (1964) 1/9 Grid designation. Everyone must be happy or at least complacent even at the cost of task accomplishment. Conflict is avoided and negative feelings are suppressed. The consultant will not confront when appropriate and will regularly suggest that members take personal "issues" off line. Dr. Feelgood uses affirmations exclusively and works to keep members "happy." Participants feel good in the short run but later are disappointed that the group has not progressed or that hidden agendas abound. |
|---|---|
| **Mr./Ms. Emoto** | Not seen today as often as in the 1970s, the Emotos came out of the T-group era and human potential movement. They focus primarily on the feelings and emotions generated in the group. Indeed, they are responsible for much of the emotion generated. They promote confrontation and encounter, not in the service of task, but for the sake of catharsis and intensity. |
| **Dr. Technique** | There is an activity available for every group situation, and Dr. Technique knows and uses them all—although frequently inappropriately. Task problems, low creativity, conflict, or silent members—regardless of the situation—the members are subjected to one activity after another. Although issues may surface, rarely are they worked through. There is a sense of playing games; Dr. Technique is more entertainer and trainer than consultant. |
| **Observer** | The Observer is laid back and makes few interventions. He or she does not confront nor offer suggestions. When asked, Observer may dispassionately describe what he or she sees, and periodically—at the end of a session—Observer may summarize. This person has little experience as a group member. This style is often seen in inexperienced consultants with little or no training. |

**Sage**

Dropping pearls of wisdom, the Sage is abstract, esoteric, and metaphorical. Somewhat aloof from the group and its members, the Sage frequently comes from an academic setting.

**Scribe**

The Scribe often brings the flip chart, sets up the room, arranges for coffee, and is always accommodating. He or she socializes with members, avoids conflict, and seems more comfortable as a support person than a consultant. The Scribe quickly volunteers to write at the flip chart, recording for the group, or finds other ways to record or take notes.

**Grand Inquisitor or Interrogator**

Asking questions, especially about others' motivations while disclosing little about self are hallmarks of the Grand Inquisitor. Group members sometimes feel they are on trial as they are interrogated relentlessly. Rather than describe behavior, the Grand Inquisitor will ask continually the *whys* of the event.

**Task Master**

The Task Master is similar to the Director but does not use maintenance interventions. He or she typically is not subtle in his or her approach. While under the guise of group process consultant, the Task Master is really the group leader. He or she becomes involved or lost in task and the content or fails to keep role boundaries managed. Members see this group process consultant as "one of us" but not in a positive sense. The members do not differentiate between themselves and the consultant. In a short time the task master has lost his or her credibility.

**Mad Bomber**

Characterized by lobbing bombs or grenades—that is, high-intensity interventions—and then totally withdrawing, the Mad Bomber lets group members manage as best they can with the damage. The interventions may be accurate, but they are at a depth the group cannot handle. Moreover, the Bomber either cannot manage the situation or is fearful of his or her own emotional involvement.

As an example, a Mad Bomber targets an anxious group member as the group is just getting started in the setting-up phase: "Harry, you look pretty nervous about being here. How do the rest of you see Harry at this point?" Having dropped his *bomb*, the consultant now waits for Harry to respond or for group members to focus in on Harry's anxiety. The Mad Bomber uses interventions in the lower right corner of the Intervention Cube (Figure 5-1), usually inappropriately and without a contract.

## The Entertainer

This group process consultant keeps the group busy, excited, and involved. Inappropriate humor, comic relief, and interesting activities may keep the members at a high pitch. However, group members do not have time to reflect, process, nor challenge themselves. Learning is kept at a minimum, and the group fails to mature.

## Pit Bull

The Pit Bull is hostile and attacks frequently. Once the Pit Bull gets on to a participant, he or she will not let go. The interventions are typically personal and punishing. Although they may grow out of the task process, they quickly generate maintenance issues. In time, group members withdraw or are reluctant to offer ideas, perceptions, or feelings for fear of attack or retaliation.

## ROOM REQUIREMENTS AND OPTIONS

Group members are expected to be effective, yet the environment and settings in which they are placed are often deplorable and counter to effective work. We need to spend more time thinking about and designing small group work environments. The following is a list of workroom variables to consider.

## Tables

Although tables are handy for binders and coffee cups, they serve as barriers to communication and "reading" people. They tend to promote psychological distance. You can see the other people only above their waist. One group replaced large tables with individual TV trays, a nice compromise.

## Chairs

Workrooms tend to have uncomfortable chairs. If employees are expected to spend time in groups, they should be comfortable while doing so.

| | |
|---|---|
| *Carpeting* | If affordable, carpeting cuts down on noise and adds to the pleasantness of the room. People tend to work better in pleasant versus sterile surroundings. |
| *Wall Space* | Adequate wall space is needed for posting flip charts with masking tape or push pins. A thin cork strip can also be added if pins are preferable and the walls must be protected. |
| *Windows* | Although not always available in many organizations, windows permit natural light and add positively to the ambiance of the room. Too much time in windowless rooms has a depressing impact. |
| *Easels and Flip Charts* | Easels and charts are the staples of the HRD, OD, and training business. They are easy to write on and publicly post. They should be of good quality and easy to tear at perforations. Although some trainers complain that graphed flip charts are for school kids, they can be quite helpful—particularly to those of us who cannot write straight or draw well. |
| *Multicolored Markers* | Colored broad-point markers keep the group stimulated and encourage creative graphics. |
| *Cork Boards* | Cork boards are essential for story boarding and wonderful for conducting creative problem solving with index cards and push pins. |
| *Chalkboard* | With the modern easel and flip chart, chalkboards are no longer common. They are handy for "chalk talks" and are, of course, erasable. However, the new electronic boards permit erasure, and more importantly, whatever is written on the board can be immediately copied. |
| *VCR, Monitor, and Camera* | There is nothing as powerful for a group as observing and examining its behavior via video. Although watching long segments is too time consuming—and often dull—focused feedback is extremely helpful. During the week, the video—with group |

members' permission—is examined by one or two members and, if possible, by someone knowledgeable in group dynamics (the task can be rotated). Not more than six "critical" incidents are extracted from the video. The whole group then watches the video segments and discusses the incidents and action steps.

The availability of a VCR is also useful for playing packaged video tapes. Likewise, if teleconferencing is considered, camera and video equipment must be available.

**Video**

Many fine group and organizational effectiveness video tapes are now available. If a group cannot own its own VCR, one can be available when needed. Be certain everyone can see the screen images. New technology in resolution now permits the use of very large screens.

**Overhead Projector**

A group should have available an overhead projector for work and presentations. Although not essential, they do promote a certain sophistication and attention to detail. However, know and test your equipment *before* group members arrive.

**Screen**

A wall can be used for projection, but a screen delivers higher luminosity and clarity of image. The screen can also be used for 35mm-slide projection.

**Telephone Outlet**

Telephones are useful for immediate communication and for conference calls. They also need to be turned off when the group is working. There is nothing as disruptive as multiple telephone calls during a meeting. This is also true of "beepers."

**Computer Projection**

Inexpensive devices that project computer images are now available. Computer-run programs can be viewed and immediate changes made to reports on word-processing programs. The current technological advances will continue to impact our own technology and delivery.

## FREQUENTLY ASKED QUESTIONS ABOUT GROUP PROCESS CONSULTATION

About five years ago, I began recording often-asked questions about group process consultation and my brief answers to those questions. More detailed explanation and rationale to many of the questions can be found throughout the text.

**Q.** *We cannot afford to have a process consultant in all our groups. What are the alternatives, and how do we decide?*

**A.** Decide which are most important, and then, using the "Eight Decision Points" (see Chapter Five), determine which are most critical to a group process consultant. A facilitator will be more appropriate for some groups. In other groups, members can be trained in some fundamental group dynamics and process skills, so they can monitor themselves.

**Q.** *Do I use "you" or "we" in my role as GPC?*

**A.** There are some subtle differences here. The group process consultant is a member of the group, although with a different role. Using "we" early on in the group can offend some members. "You," although more cautious, typically *feels* better. Once the group process consultant has established rapport and credibility, and indeed has become a member of the group, the use of "we" is more appropriate and effective.

**Q.** *It seems to me that becoming an effective process consultation is easier for an "NF" than an "ST" on the "Myers-Briggs Type Indicator." Is that accurate?*

**A.** In my experience, this is accurate. That is, the intuitive/feeler consultant prefers the "big picture" and is able to see the many interrelated group dynamics. In addition, he or she is more empathic and responsive to feelings and emotions in the group, which, of course, are the main sources of the dynamics. The "ST" group process consultant tends to be more focused on specific behaviors, is more structured, and may be put off by displays of emotional behavior. Both NFs and STs need to be aware of and work their *shadow* side appropriately.

**Q.** *How directive and assertive should I be as the GPC?*

**A.** Assertive, yes; directive, no. The GPC needs to be clear and focused in his or her interventions, but they are still offered as suggestions. By directing the group, you may get compliance, but members will not readily learn to process. They will continue to wait until you direct them. The group members may take awhile to decide whether to use your suggested intervention; but once they do, they will use it again without your help.

**Q.** *What if the group asks me to write on the flip chart?*

**A.** If you are one member in a rotation as scribe, fine. However, the role of the group process consultant is not that of scribe. You need to focus on the group and its dynamics. Scribing precludes effective focusing. Moreover, groups will frequently try to define the role of the group process consultant by adding tasks for him or her to perform. It is a way of controlling the consultant and trying to get him or her to direct the group.

**Q.** *When I enter an established group, do I negotiate a contract and ask about norms?*

**A.** Yes. One way to gain both visibility and credibility is to define your role as you understand it and then check it out with group members. Negotiating a contract is the primary way for the group process consultant to articulate what he or she does and the conditions under which he or she can best work.

Most groups do not have explicit and agreed-on behavioral work norms. The consultant can ask about norms and get members' reactions. Typically, you will need to intervene and help the group develop a set of work norms. One of the easiest ways, as indicated in an earlier chapter, is to ask the members "What makes for a lousy meeting, and what makes for a good meeting?" The members will be able to articulate what they want and do not want.

**Q.** *Should I give the group real examples of the kinds of things I do and interventions I make?*

**A.** Absolutely! The greater the accurate information available to potential clients, the more likely the client will know what to expect and the more solid the contract. All too often the group process consultant begins his or her work with the group when it does not have the slightest idea what is about to occur. When the consultant begins to intervene, particularly around maintenance dynamics, the group members resist mightily.

**Q.** *What alternatives do I have if the group members don't want me to make maintenance interventions?*

**A.** The first alternative you might consider is not to take the job. If you do, you run the risk that the group will have difficulties over which you will have no control. Moreover, the client is telling you how to do your job in ways that are ineffective and not in your nor their best interest.

You can, of course, contract for task interventions. However, it is important that group members understand the consequences of avoiding maintenance. That is, the dynamics will affect the group and could well arrest its development or performance.

**Q.** *How active should I be in the group?*

**A.** Early on, very. The group process consultant models with his or her task and maintenance interventions. The less skilled and sophisticated the group, the more active will be the consultant. During the setting-up phase of work-group activity, the consultant will be active with task interventions. During the working-at-and-through phase, maintenance interventions will increase. Over time, group members will acquire the skills to keep their group operating effectively, and the activity of the group process consultant will decrease.

**Q.** *How much assessment do I need to do before I work with the group?*

**A.** If group members understand what group process consultation is and the task/maintenance processes embedded within it, you probably will do an assessment as you work. That assessment can be conducted with the group as a whole. There will need to be a clear contract, however.

If there is a lack of knowledge about group process consultation and suspicion about you and your methods, you will probably have to spend some time gathering data with the group and individual members. Although working with the group as a whole is preferably, lack of trust and resistance may necessitate using individual data-gathering methods.

**Q.** *If the manager hires me, is he or she my client, or can the group be my client?*

**A.** I strongly believe if I am doing group or team work, the group or team is the client—regardless of who hired me! This should be made clear to the manager in the first meeting. It may make sense to work with the manager, but this would rule out your having the group as a client for group process consultation. Trying to do both blurs boundaries and generates suspicions between group members and the consultant.

**Q.** *How do I intervene in a situation in which a group member is dominating and always holding the floor? The other group members are getting angry but no one wants to say anything.*

**A.** Your question may be your most effective intervention. As an intervention it might sound something like this: "[Name], I'm aware that a few members [or name(s)] seem angry when you are speaking. I'd like to check out if it is because you are holding the floor or if it's what you are saying."

**Q.** *How about the group member who is simply negative all the time? That is, the group is moving along; everyone seems to be in agreement; but as the decision is about to be made, "Negative Ned" once again dissents.*

**A.** The intervention could be as simple as "Ned, you have been pretty negative throughout these discussions and have dissented on three of the decisions. I'd like to check out where you are and get the reactions of others in the group."

**Q.** *Then there is John, the member with a skeptical attitude who really does not want to be in the group. His manager required him to join the group. John has mentioned this previously.*

**A.** Confront John with his feelings: "I know you are pretty angry about being here and think it is a waste of time. Given

## Aphorisms

Maintenance is always in the service of the task.

An intervention said is worth a dozen unspoken.

"Here and now" is usually more impactful than "there and then."

Groups, if left on their own, gravitate to task behaviors.

The more ambiguous a task, the greater the need for maintenance.

Given the opportunity, groups will make a task more complex than is typically warranted.

A "problem" person in the group *may* be speaking for the entire group.

*Whatever* topic is discussed in the group reflects a group dynamic.

To make no contract as a group process consultant is to limit your potential effectiveness.

However a group begins, without intervention, it will probably continue until there is a crisis.

A group is as strong as its weakest member.

---

that you have stated you cannot leave, I would like to explore what you think you need to move on. We certainly think you can contribute to the group. What options do you see for becoming a contributing member—or for that matter—for dropping out? I suspect this is something you need to manage."

Of course, if the response is "I don't want to be here, and I don't have any options," an exploration of John's role in the group needs to take place. Often, the membership is not as forced as John believes, nor are the consequences for his asking out.

If John is dysfunctional and an impediment to the group—and the group cannot deal with the situation—it becomes one of those rare occasions that must be dealt with off-line.

**Q.** *When will I know if I am a group process consultant?*

**A.** When you have explained GPC in detail to a client group, have contracted for same, and are now making appropriate interventions accordingly.

**Q.** *Is task typically valued over maintenance?*

**A.** Unfortunately, yes. We live in an age of technology and information. Our major orientation is "Get the job done as quickly as you can." Public expression of even minor feelings are an anathema. Of course, they are expressed privately and behind closed doors. As a group process consultant, you must show the client group that not only are maintenance issues of major importance, the energy of the group is fueled by members' feelings.

**Q.** *When is process consultation doable?*

**A.** When the group members and manager understand and agree on a definition of group process consultation and you have a contract to do it; also when the group is small, meets regularly, and for at least an hour and a half.

**Q.** *I know that the group process consultant makes a contract; what about members?*

**A.** Yes, a contract or agreement must go both ways. The members agree that they understand group process consultation and are willing to try to be effective group members. When appropriate, all group members sign the letter of agreement or contract.

**Q.** *How can I do maintenance in my organization without being seen as "touchy-feely"?*

**A.** You might not be able to, given the organization or group. However, this is an issue that can be surfaced during the *entry* phase. Usually, when groups understand the entire process and what they are "buying" or contracting for, there are minimal problems with the touchy-feely concern.

**Q.** *The norms in my organization do not support maintenance interventions. What can I do?*

**A.** This is a tough problem—and all too common. You can first start by educating the group or team about the value of maintenance, pointing out that the energy of the group lies within its maintenance dynamics. Ask the group, "What are the typical things that lead a group to failure?" Invariably, the members will list the major cause as maintenance issues.

As for the larger organization, education is again the key—beginning with the highest executive levels. Until there is recognition and acceptance of the role of dynamics, it is unlikely there will be general acceptance of maintenance interventions.

HRD can play an important role in the education process by systematically educating various segments of the organization. Of course, this assumes that the HRD unit buys into the concept.

**Q.** *If there is a conflict between the group and one brilliant person, what do I do? Where does genius lie?*

**A.** Like all issues, this, too, belongs to the group and must be made explicit. An intervention might sound something like the following: "I am aware that there is a growing tension in the group when Jim offers a suggestion. As a group we need to understand what that is about. Thoughts, feelings, perceptions?"

**Q.** *How can I learn to say "no" in my organization to unreasonable requests and demands?*

**A.** By having confidence in your assessment of the situation and taking a consultative and collaborative approach with the manager or whomever is requesting the service. In our business, people tend to *tell* us what they want and how we should respond to that request. For example, you have probably heard something like this: "I have a group of twenty reports and I want team building for them. I have four hours on the twenty-fifth of this month. I'd like you to come in then and do it." Worse yet, how often have you responded to that request?

In this case, the consultant needs to sit down with the manager and fully explore the situation as well as a range of options if the group is too large or not ready for team building nor process consultation.

**Q.** *Can you use a group process consultant just one time?*

**A.** Technically, no. By definition, the process consultant works with a group over an extended period of time. However, one could help facilitate a group and use process skills during that time.

**Q.** *I'm the HR manager on the plant manager's staff. He has asked me to serve as GPC for his staff. What can I do?*

**A.** Explain to him that as a member of the staff you do not have the objectivity necessary for the process role. In a sense, you are an integral part of the dynamics. What is needed is someone in a role outside the group who can come in and serve as process consultant.

Some years ago, I attempted to serve as process consultant to a staff for which I was the director. Needless to say, it was a disaster. Even if I thought I knew when I was consultant and when I was director, the staff certainly could not tell. I got someone from outside our group to come in, and that worked very well.

**Q.** *What does "psychological" membership in the group mean?*

**A.** It means that you are a true member of the group, even though your role may be different than others (e.g., group process consultant). You are part of the process, relate dynamically to other members, and have a stake in the outcome. You are a part of the cohesion of the group, the glue that holds the group together. In a real way, you identify with the group and its charge.

**Q.** *Our division goes off site with fifty to seventy-five people and breaks into groups of eight to ten each. Should we have a group process consultant in each group?*

**A.** As mentioned earlier, this situation may be helped by a facilitator. A group process consultant would not have time to work the group nor meet other requirements. However, facilitators with good process skills would be invaluable.

**Q.** *Is a person inherently a good group process consultant?*

**A.** Some people do seem to be *naturals*. They tend to be warm, relate well, and have a high level of intuition. They are able to *see* dynamics at multilevels simultaneously and remember observed behavior patterns. Although these characteristics can also be learned by many people, there are those consultants who are so concrete that they rely solely on techniques and not themselves as the agents of change.

**Q.** *Can group process consultation work for a group of bonus-level executives with a staff position GPC—especially in a company that emphasizes hierarchy?*

**A.** Certainly, but the GPC would have to follow the flow model carefully. That is, the group would need to understand exactly what group process consultation is about and the GPC's honest reservations about conducting it from his or her role and position. Then, a clear and explicit contract would need to be agreed-on by all. If the contract was frequently violated, the GPC might need to recontract.

**Q.** *I consult to a large group (about eighteen) of senior managers. I have a good contract with the group. I can do pretty much what I want to in terms of interventions, and so on. Nevertheless, it is tough to get agreement on anything. We are at a turning point in the project. That is, a decision on an approach for data analysis needs to be made. One senior manager, in particular, tries to dominate the meetings. Any suggestions?*

**A.** As you know by now, getting consensus in a group this large is all put impossible under the best of circumstances. Once the members have the data-analysis options they need, break the group into three subgroups of six members each. The subgroups can work toward consensus. Then, one member from each subgroup (with full power) meets together privately to work on a final consensus.

Another method is to suggest a quorum vote, if the group agrees to this. That is, the group will work for a specified time on a task and attempt to reach consensus. If they cannot, and if a quorum—perhaps three-quarters of the group—is in agreement, the action carries. The group, of course, must agree to this technique in advance. Although it works against consensus, it is an effective tool for large groups and those groups with a member or two who continually work against consensus because of their own needs.

The rule of thumb here is to break the large group into more manageable units, yet keeping them all informed and in contact as much as possible. As for your dominating senior manager, the situation must be confronted directly, yet not in a punitive way. Sometimes an intervention such as "I want to do a quick check and see if folks feel that everyone has an opportunity to contribute" usually brings out concerns about monopolists.

**Q.** *My group is composed primarily of task-oriented people who think they value maintenance; but when conflict arises, they quickly switch into a task mode—thus stifling any expression of feelings. Conflict simmers under the surface and occasionally arises in angry comments seemingly unrelated to the real issue.*

**A.** Your description may well be the effective intervention; that is, a behavior description based on your observation and then an interpretation about what happens to the feelings in the group. This should prompt the group members to talk about what is happening.

**Q.** *The group I'm working with is polite with underlying currents of hostility not being addressed.*

**A.** As in the previous example, often our best intervention is our observation and description of the dynamic. For example, "Let me check out an observation. There seems to be a lot of what I call *surface politeness* here. I have a hunch that some of you are pretty ticked off about [issue] and have not been willing to talk about it. What do you think?"

**Q.** *The group has met on a task for some months and is now bogged down. Attendance is also spotty and there is no apparent ownership of the task. Suggestions?*

**A.** Once again, describe the situation: "You've been meeting for two months now and are obviously bogged down. In addition, attendance is spotty and from my vantage point, no one nor the group is taking ownership for the task. First of all, do you agree with my observation? If so, maybe we ought to spend some quality time talking about what is going on in here."

**Q.** *In a division meeting to discuss a budget that is too small, senior officers are pulling rank and stopping the process by making what seems like speeches.*

**A.** As an external group process consultant—with the right kind of contract—you can "call the game" and confront the situation directly. However, realistically, if you are internal and your position is not secure, you may have to employ other means, such as doing a quick process check by distributing index cards and asking people to write down what they think is happening. You then quickly read them anonymously. People will describe accurately what is transpiring. You then say, "Given that these comments are accurate, let me suggest the following procedure..."

**Q.** *What about a passive member who, when pressed to participate, consistently plays the role of "devil's advocate"?*

**A.** That often happens. The member when pressed sees his or her role as the challenger. One, I think this can be pointed out as an observation. However, it may well be that the person does not feel he or she is a "member" of the group, or has some anger about how he or she has been treated. All of these possibilities can be checked out, as long as it is done gently and with the person's—and group's—best interests in mind.

**Q.** *My boss is long winded and becomes ineffective when he tries to represent his section's interest at meetings. I would like to help him become more effective and less judgmental or threatening. How might I do this?*

**A.** This does not sound like an issue for a group process consultant. Depending on your relationship with him and his willingness to receive and use feedback, meet with him off line and share your perception. Remember the feedback guidelines: Ask him if he is would like your observations about him. Describe the behaviors, without intensity, and what you think is the impact. Suggest he check it out with others, and ask him if he thinks you might be of help to him.

**Q.** *One member objects to discussing feelings in the group and insists we should get on with the task. What do you suggest?*

**A.** First, you will need to check out what is behind the behavior. You might suggest that discussing appropriate feelings have everything to do with the task, and check where the rest of the group is. If you have a contract, you might revisit it and ask the group if they wish to renegotiate. It may well be that the member is fearful about emotions getting out of control or that the group spends too much time on maintenance and not enough explicitly on task. The group process consultant here needs to be careful not to ignore or override the group member in focus. This is particularly true of more maintenance-oriented consultants.

**Q.** *Some members are vying for influence in the group. Two members continually struggle for leadership and control. This affects the group in that other members are not listened to because of so much energy going into the struggle.*

**A.** Use the Intervention Cube (Figure 5-1). This situation usually calls for a direct intervention, interpersonal, behavior description/interpretive, medium to high intensity, and Level III in depth. If this does not get all the members discussing the process, well....

**Q.** *Two competing groups have been reorganized into one. The senior management team members are working in different directions and blaming each other for the ineffectiveness of the organization.*

**A.** This is a systemic issue and requires an organizational consultant rather than a group process consultant. If a consultant had not been brought in *before* the reorganization, as seems to be the case, an option is to have one work with the *new* group to work out these issues. Since the group is already in place, consider—after contracting—meeting with the members and conducting a group assessment, including prioritization of issues and "where do we go next?" action steps. When this is in place, the group process consultant is then in a position to work with the group over time, which is probably needed.

**Q.** *My group has neither task nor maintenance skills, yet the members are eager and want me as a group process consultant. Should I accept?*

**A.** You are lucky! Consider a program whereby they can learn some skills around both task process and maintenance. Start first with task and see that the group learns how to rotate roles, set agendas, acquire a problem-solving sequence, and so on. As maintenance issues arise, plug in maintenance-skill acquisition activities. When the group is ready, you can then move on to working with them as a group process consultant. If you are able to have someone else conduct the training, your role will remain clear and clean.

**Q.** *The group manager stifles creativity by comments like "That's great, but the technicians will never buy it." He treats his group members as children who need their tasks to be "simple." How should I deal with this situation?*

**A.** As mentioned previously, often the best intervention is to articulate the problem effectively. For example, "Jack, I want to run something by you and the group. You know, if I were on the receiving end of your comments, I would feel like a kid who needs everything made simple. I wonder what that does to creativity here? Where are all of you with that?"

**Q.** *The manager is an "ENFP" who uses her relationship skills to manipulate and control her staff. She goes to extremes to maintain appearances. She advocates harmony but still does everything her way; for example, she will not hold many meetings. When she does, she will do all the talking. There is no follow-through, no minutes, nor action items.*

**A.** I would rather focus on the manager's behaviors than the ENFP factor. If this manager agreed to a group process consultant, then her behavior needs to be confronted by you or group members. If you are not the group process consultant, but have access to her in a consultative way, ask if she would like to hear some of your observations and the possible impact of her actions. If she does, then give them to her *behaviorally.* I trust you would be available to help her further in working on actions.

**Q.** *I have to deal with an overly dominant member in my group setting. He ends up setting direction because he holds the purse strings. Others merely submit.*

**A.** The question is why this issue has not been raised and openly discussed in then group. You can choose to raise it directly as a hypothesis you have. Or you could draw a carpet (rug) on the flip chart; then ask members to jot down on Post-it™ notes what they think is being *swept under the rug* in the group and to stick the notes on the rug. Once the issues are stuck on the flip chart—and it is unusual for none to be put there—give each member three different-colored stick-on dots and ask them to indicate their top priorities (what they should deal with first, second, and third) by placing the dots on the flip chart on the issues that had been swept under the rug. Then deal with what is up there.

## COMMON MISTAKES AND PITFALLS

I am frequently asked by participants in workshops to name the most common mistakes and pitfalls made by group process consultants. The following twenty-five mistakes and pitfalls are shared by beginners and experienced practitioners:

1. Focusing on results too soon versus taking a continuous problem-oriented approach.

2. Not checking immediately and periodically to determine how members *feel* about working on the task at hand.

3. Not determining if there is group agreement regarding the problem to be solved, product to be produced, or service to be delivered.

4. Encouraging or allowing a group member to immediately move to the flip chart to record data without first clearly defining the problem.

5. Talking too much or too little.

6. Not having a clear and accepted contract with the group.

7. Not having a problem-solving sequence in your "kit."

8. Uttering truisms (e.g., "I notice that you haven't spoken, Mary.").

9. Not checking for reactions to the environment in which the group members are working.

10. Talking too long.

11. Over-explaining an intervention.

12. Defending an intervention.

13. Not looking directly at people when you are making an intervention.

14. Taking issues off line.

15. Not trusting your gut.

16. Not willing to *risk* an intervention.

17. Too much task, too little maintenance.

18. Too much maintenance, little or no task.

19. Colluding in scapegoating a group member.

20. Playing favorites because of perceived power, sexual attraction, or possible professional favors.

21. Getting drawn into the content.

22. Evaluating and not describing in terms of effectiveness.

23. Not listening.

24. Not using your intuition and instincts.

25. Not trusting group process.

## RULES OF THUMB FOR THE PROCESS CONSULTANT

| Do's | Don'ts |
|---|---|
| Contract with group re role | Suggest voting for role selection (e.g., leader) |
| Suggest procedures and roles (e.g., agenda, steps, scribe, etc.) | Excuse yourself for intervening |
| Be assertive | Be directive |
| Suggest | Scribe, time keep, or record |
| Use here-and-now interventions | Suggest brainstorming in a large group |
| Suggest brainstorming as an individual then gather information via the nominal group technique | Overuse there-and-then interventions |
| Look interested and enthusiastic | Always think the group must stay in that configuration |
| Work collaboratively | Suggest consensus in a group larger than 12 |
| Be concrete and specific | Be abstract |
| Balance task and maintenance | Make things more complex than they are |
| Behave now; pay later | "Explain" your interventions |
| Sit as a *member* of the group | Sit outside as an observer |
| Suggest | Use "should" |
| Talk less versus more | Use more than two brief sentences at a time |
| Show warmth and caring | Give advice |
| Be alert and carefully observe | Direct or lead |
| Recognize your own mistakes | Defend |

| | |
|---|---|
| Remember repeated behaviors and patterns | Serve as scribe |
| Be patient | Take copious notes |
| Give multiple options | Assume anything |
| Match (about 5% less) the group member's intensity | Recap or summarize for late comers |
| Offer behavioral data | Use "psychological" explanations |
| Listen to your intuition | Take sides |
| Describe behaviors | Ask "why?" |

## Executive Planning Team ♦ ♦ ♦

As members of the executive planning team reached milestones, they celebrated together and at times with other appropriate units and groups. They attended some ball games and had two dinners together with wives or friends. At the meeting after the second dinner, Vic cautiously raised the potential hindrance of their being an all-male group. Bill added, "And a macho group at that!" Although there was sentiment that there was enough *diversity* in this group, the comment opened another level of discussion the group had not previously experienced.

Their planning work and tenure almost completed, action steps and implementation occupied much of the group's time. Task interventions from Scott increased. Maintenance issues were less frequent until the last few meetings. Scott found the group once again resistant to discussing two key maintenance issues—closure and closeness. The termination of the group was a bit easier to manage for the members than was how they felt about their work and one another. Scott asked each of them to develop metaphors about their feelings and time together. Bill responded with the following metaphor:

## Macho to the End

We were a Marine squad that had to take a key hill with only small arms. We were cut off from our platoon and had to improvise. We couldn't have done it if we weren't real close and didn't trust one another. But we pulled it off—and without any casualties. We have a great feeling of camaraderie here toward each other, real buddies. And we took the [expletive deleted] hill!

That was about as sentimental as the team got, but it was enough for them to deal with their feelings and bring closure to the group. The team also took the last day to "celebrate" and to affirm Scott for the work he had done as the group process consultant.

*Epilogue*     Members of the Executive Planning Team were very successful in their planning. They set into motion a concerted effort by the entire organization to bring about a breakthrough in their business. They eventually regained their market share. All but two members continued to be effective now with their own staffs, as well as on other teams and committees. They also became proponents of group process consultation for important teams. Unfortunately, the two who were least effective on the team likewise continued in that vein. One, however, was quick to use the HRD department to help him manage his own staff meetings.

## *Quality Circles* ♦ ♦ ♦

*Circle I.* Circle I worked hard at its new challenge. Phil offered that since they were doing so well with their processing, they might rotate that role as they had others. He added, "As long as Kim doesn't mind or think we're taking her job away." Kim admitted she felt a bit uncomfortable but felt it was another growth step for the group. She said she would serve as back-up.

Phil was first in the role, which initially proved to be awkward. He got involved in the content while process consultant and presented himself in role as director. Group members, however, quickly pointed out his faux pas and Phil pulled back. With Kim's help Phil responded to his GPC role quite well. Too well, perhaps. When it was suggested another member start practice in the role, Phil balked and resisted. Group pressure was exerted and Phil passed the role to Ruby. Over the next few months all but Sheila and Rob took their turn. Neither Sheila nor Rob had the interest (and probably not the capability). This was acceptable to the group members who earlier agreed that GPC training was optional.

Circle I ended with final presentations to management and a Friday-afternoon "pizza and pop" celebration. They managed the ending only fairly well, congratulating themselves and being pleased seemingly more for members' personal and professional growth than for their contribution to the company.

*Circle II.* Circle II knew the group would soon have to end. Two members were transferred to another division. Curiously, Michael's job was in jeopardy because of downsizing. However, his reputation as a group leader enabled him to move into a newly created HRD position, which included training group leaders and company facilitators in group process consultation.

The final few weeks were difficult for the group members. They had come a long way over the year and a half of their existence. With consultation from an external OD consultant, Michael discussed termination and celebration with the group. Humor as comic relief punctuated their last meeting, as members awkwardly gave their kudos and appreciation to one another. Later that week, members arranged a dinner celebration for themselves with spouses or friends. The HRD manager was also on hand to thank the group for its work and a confession that she really did not think any quality team would survive more than a month. One of the three, of course, had not survived. The dinner celebration ended on a high note of satisfaction and pride for a job well done.

## Epilogue

The success of two of three quality teams generated ten others. Yet, the message of the value of both task and maintenance processes were not heard by upper management, despite consultation with the manager of HRD, Kim, and Michael. Fortunately, Michael—in his new position—was able to influence the training design.

Some members of both Kim's and Michael's teams were trained as circle leaders. Others were selected for other committee and group-membership roles.

## Hospital Administration ♦ ♦ ♦

Critical changes have been made throughout the hospital. Unfortunately, cuts also had to be made; some personnel were lost. A leaner hospital is now competitive in the community. The consumer, for the first time, is central. The executive group has added new members; however, all but one of the original group remain. They had to manage that transition also. At times the old group looks back with laughter and nostalgia at its early struggles and efforts. The members acknowledged the contribution of Laura in getting them started and keeping them focused. Laura had terminated as group process consultant when she moved to another state. However, Laura kept in telephone contact and was invited to celebrate the opening of a new clinic.

*Epilogue*

The process begun, not so long ago, is well established in the hospital. Not only are there problem-solving groups everywhere, self-directed teams have also started in some units. Most important, there seems to be a common *process* language and norms. It is "O.K." to talk about how you feel and to raise the concerns you have. Certainly, some people have taken advantage of the norms, but others remind and challenge them. There is also heard much more affirmation and support.

# References

Ackerman, L.S. (1986, December). Development, transition or transformation: The question of change in organizations. *OD Practitioner, 18*(4), 1-8.

Argyris, C. (1970). *Intervention theory & method.* Reading, MA: Addison-Wesley.

Argyris, C., & Schon, D. (1974). *Theory in practice.* San Francisco, CA: Jossey-Bass.

Bales, R.F. (1950). *Interaction process analysis.* Chicago: University of Chicago Press.

Bales, R.F., & Cohen, S.P. (1979). *SYMLOG: A system for the multiple level observation of groups.* New York: The Free Press.

Beck, A.C., & Hillmar, E.D. (1986). *Positive management practices.* San Francisco, CA: Jossey-Bass.

Bennis, W.G. (1966). *Changing organizations.* New York: McGraw-Hill.

Bennis, W., & Shepard, H. (1948). A theory of group development. *Human Relations, 1,* 314-320.

Blake, R.R., & Mouton, J.S. (1964). *The managerial grid.* Houston, TX: Gulf Publishing Co.

Blake, R.R., & Mouton, J.S. (1983). *Consultation: A handbook for individual and organization development* (2nd ed.). Reading, MA: Addison-Wesley.

Block, P. (1981). *Flawless consulting: A guide to getting your expertise used.* San Diego, CA: Pfeiffer & Company.

Block, P. (1987). *The empowered manager: Positive political skills at work.* San Francisco, CA: Jossey-Bass.

Bouchard, T.J., Jr. (1972). Training, motivation, and personality as determinants of the effectiveness of brainstorming groups and individuals. *Journal of Applied Psychology, 4,* 324-331.

Bradford, D.L., & Cohen, A.R. (1984). *Managing for excellence.* New York: John Wiley & Sons.

Bransford, J.D., & Stein, B.S. (1984). *The ideal problem solver.* New York: W.H. Freeman and Company.

Brown, L.D. (1983). *Managing conflict at organizational interfaces.* Reading, MA: Addison-Wesley.

Bushe, G.R., & Gibbs, B.W. (1990). Predicting organization development consulting competence from the Myers-Briggs Type Indicator and stage of ego development. *The Journal of Applied Behavioral Science, 26*(3), 337-357.

Clapp, N.W. (1980). *Work group norms: Leverage for organizational change theory and application.* Plainfield, NJ: Block, Petrella, Weisbord.

Cohen, A.M., & Smith, R.D. (1976). *The critical incident in growth groups.* San Diego, CA: Pfeiffer & Company.

Committee on Techniques for the Enhancement of Human Performance/Commission on Behavioral and Social Sciences and Education/National Research Council. (1991). Enhancing human performance. In D. Druckman & R.A. Bjork (Eds.), *In the mind's eye* (pp. 12-18). Washington, DC: National Academy Press.

Crum, T.F. (1987). *The magic of conflict.* New York: Simon and Schuster.

Deal, T.E., & Kennedy, A.A. (1982). *Corporate cultures: The rites and rituals of corporate life.* Reading, MA: Addison-Wesley.

Dexter, L.A. (1970). *Elite and specialized interviewing.* San Francisco, CA: Jossey-Bass.

Dunham, R.B., & Smith, F.J. (1979). *Organizational surveys: An internal assessment of organizational health.* Glenview, IL: Scott, Foresman.

Dunnette, M.D., Campbell, J.P., & Jaastad, K. (1963). The effect of group participation on brainstorming effectiveness for two industrial samples. *Journal of Applied Psychology, 47,* 30-37.

Filley, A.C. (1975). *Interpersonal conflict resolution.* Glenview, IL: Scott, Foresman.

Fisher, B.A. (1974). *Small group decision making: Communication and the group process.* New York: McGraw-Hill.

Fisher, R., & Ury, W. (1981). *Getting to yes.* Boston, MA: Houghton Mifflin.

Forsyth, D.R. (1990). *Group dynamics.* Pacific Grove, CA: Brooks/Cole.

Fox, W.M. (1987). *Effective group problem solving.* San Francisco, CA: Jossey-Bass.

Gellermann, W. (1985). Values and ethical issues for human systems development practitioners. In R. Tannenbaum, N. Margulis, F. Massarik, & Associates (Eds.), *Human systems development.* San Francisco, CA: Jossey-Bass.

Gersick, C.J.G. (1988). Time and transition in work teams: Toward a new model of group development. *Academy of Management Journal, 31,* 9-41.

Goffman, E. (1973). *The presentation of self in everyday life.* Woodstock, NY: Overlook Press.

Goodstein, J., & Goodstein, L.D. (1991). A matrix for evaluating training. In J.W. Pfeiffer (Ed.), *The 1991 annual: Developing human resources.* San Diego, CA: Pfeiffer & Company.

Goodstein, L. (1978). *Consulting with human services.* Reading, MA: Addison-Wesley.

Goodstein, L.D., Cooke, P., & Goodstein, J. (1983). The team orientation and behavior inventory (TOBI). In L.D. Goodstein & J.W. Pfeiffer (Eds.), *The 1983 annual for facilitators, trainers, and consultants.* San Diego, CA: Pfeiffer & Company.

Goodstein, L.D., Nolan, T.M., & Pfeiffer, J.W. (1992). *Applied strategic planning: A comprehensive guide.* San Diego, CA: Pfeiffer & Company.

Gordon, W.J.J. (1961). *Synectics.* New York: Harper & Row.

Gray, B. (1989). *Collaborating: Finding common ground for multiparty problems.* San Francisco, CA: Jossey-Bass.

Grove, D.A., & Ostroff, C. (1990). Program evaluation. In K. Wexley and J. Hinrichs (Eds.), *Developing human resources.* Washington, DC: BNA Books.

Hackman, J.R. (1983). *A normative model of work team effectiveness* (Tech. Rep. No. 2). New Haven, CT: Yale School of Organization and Management.

Hamilton, E.E. (1988). The facilitation of organizational change: An empirical study of factors predicting change agents' effectiveness. *The Journal of Applied Behavioral Science, 24*(1), 37-59.

Hanson, P.G. (1972). What to look for in groups: An observation guide. In J.W. Pfeiffer & J.E. Jones (Eds.), *The 1972 annual handbook for group facilitators.* San Diego, CA: Pfeiffer & Company.

Harrison, R. (1970). Choosing the depth of organizational intervention. *The Journal of Applied Behavioral Science, 6*(2), 181-202.

Hart, L. (1981). *Learning from conflict: A handbook for trainers and group leaders.* Reading, MA: Addison-Wesley.

Heider, J. (1985). *The tao of leadership.* Atlanta, GA: Humanics New Age.

Huse, E.F. (1980). *Organization development and change.* St. Paul, MN: West Publishing Co.

Jacobs, A. (1974). The use of feedback in groups. In A. Jacobs & W.W. Spradlin (Eds.), *The group as the agent of change.* New York: Behavioral Publications.

Jacobs, M., Jacobs, A., Feldman, G., & Cavior, N. (1973). Feedback II: The 'credibility gap': Delivery of positive and negative and emotional and behavioral feedback in groups. *Journal of Consulting and Clinical Psychology, 41,* 215-223.

Jacobs, M., Jacobs, A., Gatz, M., & Schaible, T. (1973). Credibility and desirability of positive and negative structured feedback in groups. *Journal of Consulting and Clinical Psychology, 40,* 244-252.

Kelley, C.A. (1975). Guidelines for critiquing a training presentation. *Small-group training theory and practice: Workshop participant book.* San Diego, CA: Pfeiffer & Company.

Kelley, C.A. (1975). Training session critique form. *Small-group training theory and practice: Workshop participant book.* San Diego, CA: Pfeiffer & Company.

Kellogg, D.M. (1984). Contrasting successful and unsuccessful OD consultation relationships. *Group & Organization Studies, 9*(2), 151-176.

Kerr, N.L. (1989). Illusions of efficacy: The effects of group size on perceived efficacy in social dilemmas. *Journal of Experimental Social Psychology, 25,* 287-313.

Kilmann, R. (1984). *Beyond the quick fix: Managing five tracks to organizational success.* San Francisco, CA: Jossey-Bass.

Kirkpatrick, D.L. (1959). Techniques for evaluating training programs. *Journal of the American Society of Training Directors, 13,* 3-9, 21-26.

Kirkpatrick, D.L. (1960). Techniques for evaluating training programs. *Journal of the American Society of Training Directors, 14,* 13-18, 28-32.

Kirkpatrick, D.L. (1967). Evaluation of training. In R.L. Craig & L.R. Bittel (Eds.), *Training and development handbook.* New York: McGraw-Hill.

Koberg, D., & Bagnall, J. (1981). *The all new universal traveler.* Los Altos, CA: William Kaufmann, Inc.

Kreeger, L.E. (1975). *The large group: Dynamics and therapy.* Itasca, IL: F.E. Peacock.

Latane, B., Williams, K., & Harkins, S. (1979). Many hands make light the work: The causes and consequences of social loafing. *Journal of Personality and Social Psychology, 37,* 822-832.

LeShan, L. (1974). *How to meditate: A guide to self-discovery.* New York: Bantam Books.

Levinson, H. (1977, June). Managing psychological man. *Management Review,* pp. 121-133.

Lewin, K. (1951). *Field theory in social science.* New York: Harper.

Lindaman, E.B., & Lippitt, R.O. (1979). *Choosing the future you prefer: A goal setting guide.* Washington, DC: Development Publications.

Locke, E.A., & Latham, G.P. (1984). *Goal setting: A motivational technique that works!* Englewood Cliffs, NJ: Prentice-Hall.

Locke, E.A., & Latham, G.P. (1990). *A theory of goal setting and task performance.* Englewood Cliffs, NJ: Prentice Hall.

Luft, J., Kingsbury, S., & Schrader, H. (1990, April). Shared concerns: Psychometrics in human interaction. *NTL News & Views,* pp. 10-12.

Maier, N.R.F. (1963). *Problem-solving discussions and conferences.* New York: McGraw-Hill.

McCall, G.J., & Simmons, J.L. (Eds.). (1969). *Issues in participant observation: A text and reader.* Reading, MA: Addison-Wesley.

McGonagle, J.J. (1981). *Managing the consultant.* Radnor, PA: Chilton Book Company.

McGonagle, J.J. (1982). *Business agreements: A complete guide to oral and written contracts.* Radnor, PA: Chilton Book Company.

Michalko, M. (1991). *Thinkertoys.* Berkeley, CA: Ten Speed Press.

Moore, C. (1986). *The mediation process.* San Francisco, CA: Jossey-Bass.

Moosbruker, J. (1989, March). The consultant as process leader. *OD Practitioner, 21,* 10-12.

Myers, I.B. (1980). *Gifts differing.* Palo Alto, CA: Consulting Psychologists Press.

Nadler, D.A. (1977). *Feedback and organization development: Using data-based methods.* Reading, MA: Addison-Wesley.

Osborn, A.F. (1963). *Applied imagination.* New York: Scribner's.

Ott, J.S. (1989). *The organizational culture perspective.* Chicago: The Dorsey Press.

Patton, M.Q. (1981). *Creative evaluation.* Newbury Park, CA: Sage Publications.

Pfeiffer, J.W., Heslin, R., & Jones, J.E. (1973). *Instrumentation in human relations training.* San Diego, CA: Pfeiffer & Company.

Pneuman, R.W., & Bruehl, M.E. (1982). *Managing conflict: A complete process-centered handbook.* Englewood Cliffs, NJ: Prentice-Hall.

Reddy, W.B. (1969). "Reflections." Unpublished poem.

Reddy, W.B. (1985). The role of the change agent in the future of group work. *The Journal for Specialists in Group Work, 10*(2), 103-107.

Reddy, W.B. (in press). Interventions in small groups. In W.J. Rothwell, R. Sullivan, & G.N. McLean (Eds.), *Facilitating organizational change: The theory and practice of organizational development.* San Diego, CA: Pfeiffer & Company.

Reddy, W.B., & Phillips, C. (1992). Traditional assessment: The way of the dinosaur. *OD Practitioner, 24*(4), 1-2.

Robert, M. (1982). *Managing conflict from the inside out.* San Diego, CA: Learning Associates/Pfeiffer & Company.

Schaible, T.D., & Jacobs, A. (1975). Feedback III: Sequence effects enhancement of feedback acceptance and group attractiveness by manipulation of the sequence and valance of feedback. *Small Group Behavior, 6,* 151-173.

Schein, E.H. (1961). *Coercive persuasion.* New York: W.W. Norton & Company.

Schein, E.H. (1979). Personal changes through interpersonal relationships. In W. Bennis, J. Van Maanen, E.H. Schein, & F.I. Steele (Eds.), *Essays in interpersonal dynamics.* Homewood, IL: Dorsey Press.

Schein, E.H. (1985). *Organizational culture and leadership.* San Francisco, CA: Jossey-Bass.

Schein, E.H. (1987). *Process consultation: Vol. II: Lessons for managers and consultants.* Reading, MA: Addison-Wesley.

Schein, E.H. (1988). *Process consultation: Vol. I: Its role in organization development* (2nd ed.). Reading, MA: Addison-Wesley.

Schein, E.H. (1990, Spring). A general philosophy of helping: Process consultation. *Sloan Management Review,* pp. 57-64.

Schein, E.H., & Bennis, W.G. (1965). *Personal and organizational change through group methods: The laboratory approach.* New York: John Wiley & Sons.

Schutz, W.C. (1958). *FIRO: A three-dimensional theory of interpersonal behavior.* New York: Holt, Rinehart and Winston.

Schutz, W.C. (1967). *Joy: Expanding human awareness.* New York: Grove Press.

Schutz, W.C. (1971). *Here comes everybody.* New York: Harper & Row.

Seashore, C.N., Seashore, E.W., & Weinberg, G.M. (1991). *What did you say? The art of giving and receiving feedback.* North Attleborough, MA: Douglas Charles Press.

Shaw, M.E. (1981). *Group dynamics: The psychology of small group behavior.* New York: McGraw-Hill.

Simon, A., & Boyer, E.G. (Eds.). (1974). *Mirrors for behavior III: An anthology of observation instruments.* Wyncote, PA: Communication Materials Center.

Srivastva, S., Cooperrider, D.L., & Associates (1990). *Appreciative management and leadership: The power of positive thought and action in organizations.* San Francisco, CA: Jossey-Bass.

Tannen, D. (1990). *You just don't understand: Women and men in conversation.* New York: William Morrow.

Tubbs, S.L. (1992). *A systems approach to small group interaction.* New York: Random House.

Tuckman, B. (1965). Developmental sequence in small groups. *Psychological Bulletin, 63,* 384-399.

VanGundy, A.B. (1981). *Techniques of structured problem solving.* New York: Van Nostrand Reinhold.

Weick, K. (1979). Cognitive processes in organizations. In B. Straw (Ed.), *Research in organizational behavior.* Greenwich, CT: Jai.

Weisbord, M.R. (1987). *Productive workplaces: Organizing and managing for dignity, meaning, and community.* San Francisco, CA: Jossey-Bass.

Whitaker, D.S., & Lieberman, M.A. (1964). *Psychotherapy through the group process.* New York: Atherton Press.

Zechmeister, E.B., & Nyberg, S.E. (1982). *Human memory: An introduction to research and theory.* Pacific Grove, CA: Brooks/Cole.

# Index

Deal, T.E., 56

Decision-making, 123
  strategies for, 153–154

Definition, 60, 62

Demos, 182–183

Dependence-submission stage, 117

De-skilling, 34

Developmental change, 144

Developmental plan, 163–164

Dexter, L.A., 150

Director, 189

Disclosure, 176

Disenchantment-fight, 122

Diversity, 173
  management of, 161

Dr. Feelgood, 190

Dr. Technique, 190

Dunham, R.B., 155

Dunnette, M.D., 155

Dynamics, 145
  consultants and, 17
  of group, 32–33
  iceberg of, 92, 103
  and intervention depth and selection, 106
  of large group, 9
  Level I, 94
  Level II, 94, 98, 99
  Level III, 94–97, 98, 99
  Level IV, 97, 98–99
  levels of, 92–94
    in working-at-and-through phase, 125
  Level V, 98
  specific to group process consultation, 146
  ten clues to, 88–91

Dysfunctional behavior, 139

**E**

Easels, 193

Eberle, R., 155

Education, 48–49, 184-185

Education. *See also* Entry Education
  entry and, 14–15
  and initial contract, 48

Electronic mail, 183

E-mail. *See* Electronic mail

Emergent norms, 33

Emotional/reflective interventions, 83, 84–85, 85, 87–88, 98, 106

Emotions, expressing, 145

Enacted environments, 31–32

Enchantment-flight, 122

Endorsement, 62

Energy, 90

Entertainer, 192

Entry. *See also* Group process consultation; Contract; Education; Assessment components of, 43–44

Equifinality, 11

Ethics, 167–168, 173–175
  accountability and responsibility, 176–178
  contracts and, 175
  disclosure and, 176
  of evaluation, 178
  and information access, 175–176
  issues with group members, 176

Hart, L., 156

Heider, J., 11

Helping and collaboration model, and philosophy of group process consultation, 9

Here-and-now interventions, 106–108

Heslin, R., 150

High performance, 169–170

Hillmar, E.D., 70

Honesty, 171

Hospital administration
balance of focus, 37
consultant skills and, 166
and dynamics and intervention types, 110–111
entering work proper, 80
and entry, 66
epilogue, 211–212
and group process consultation, 6, 25
group process consultation embedded in, 187
processes and, 30
and work group activity phases, 138–140

HRD. *See* Human resource development

Human-interaction groups, 158

Human resource development, responsibilities in organization, 178–185

Humor, 157
use of, 91

Huse, E.F., 2

I-Ching, 10

Inclusion, 95, 117, 117

Information, access to, 175–176

Instruments
for assessment, 52
and group assessment via group, 152
and group assessment via individuals, 150–151

Insularity, 186

Intensity, of intervention, 83–85

Interaction, within groups, 7

Internal membership, 18
of consultant, 21
of facilitator, 20
of leader, 20
of manager, 19

Interpersonal change, 144

Interpersonal needs, 97

Interpersonal relationships, maintenance and, 28

Interpretation interventions, 83, 84–85, 87–88, 98–99, 106

Interrogator, 191

Intervention, 17. *See also* specific types
appropriateness of, 84
in closure, termination, and celebration phase, 133–135
consultant's role and, 9
defined, 7
depth of, 92
choosing, 100–103
and group types, 103–105
early, 38–41
effective, 22

**J**

**K**

**L**

and task, 126–127
Protection
from others, 177–178
from self, 177
Psychological mindedness,
102–103
Purpose. *See* Mission

## Q

Quality circles
balance of focus, 37
consultant skills and,
165–166
and dynamics and intervention types, 108–110
entering work proper, 78–79
and entry, 64–66
epilogue, 211–212
and group process consultation, 6, 25
group process consultation
embedded in, 186–187
processes and, 29–30
and work group activity
phases, 137–138
Quasi-structured interview, 53
Questionnaire, 53–54
Quorum, 154

## R

Reddy, W.B., 142, 150, 157,
158
Reinforcement, 144
Resistance
and intervention types, 84
and norms, 56
Resolution, 122

Respect
for group rights, 169
for sponsor, 170
Responsibility, 176–178
Risk, 172
and intervention types, 84
Robert, M., 156
Role
of consultant, 11, 18
and intervention, 9
distinctions of, 18–24
of facilitator, 20
of leader, 19–20
of manager, 18–19
Room
requirements of, 192–194
setup and intervention, 14

## S

Sage, 191
SCAMPER, 155
Scapegoating, 177–178
Schaible, T., 160
Schein, E.H., 2, 8, 10, 28, 56,
75, 144
Schon, D., 76
Schrader, 151
Schutz, W.C., 31, 94, 95, 96,
113, 117, 122, 130
Scribe, 191
Scribing, 196
Seashore, C.N., 159
Seashore, E.W., 159
Secrecy, 57
Self, use of, 86
Self-knowledge, 143–144,
157–158, 175

T-groups, 105
Theory, 143, 144–145
  change, 144–145
  espoused v. in-use, 1, 76
  learning, 144
There-and-then interventions, 106
TOBI. *See* Team Orientation and Behavior Inventory
Tone, 89
Tracking, 90
Training
  as behavioral skill, 148–149
  design considerations, 148–149
  style considerations, 148–149
Transformational change, 144
Transitional change, 144
Tubbs, S.L., 145, 154
Tuckman, B., 113, 117, 122

## U

Unconscious, 92–93, 98
Ury, W., 156

## V

Values, 69–71, 73–74, 159, 167–168
  behavior, 171
  collaboration, 168–169
  competence, 170–171
  conflict, 172–173
  of consultant, 61, 62
  diversity, 173
  group v. individual needs, 172
  high performance, 169–170
  honesty, 171
  member-perceived, 54
  personal satisfaction, 169
  ranking, 72
  respect, 169, 170
  risk taking, 172
  spirit of inquiry, 168
  task-maintenance balance, 171
VanGundy, A.B., 68
Videos, 183, 194. *See also* Camera equipment
Vision, 9, 16, 38, 69–71, 73–74, 153
Visioning, 70

## W

Wall space, 193
Weick, K., 31
Weinberg, G.M., 159
Weisbord, M.R., 58, 181
WES. *See* Work Environment Scale
Whitaker, D.S., 28, 107
Williams, K., 9, 32
Windows, 193
Work Environment Scale (WES), 52
Work-group activity, four phases of, 113–116
Working-at-and-through phase, 114–115, 121-122
  consultant behavior in, 124
  interventions in, 124–125
  and maintenance, 123–124
  and task, 122–123
Work proper, 67, 74–75

# Colophon

Editor: Mary Harper Kitzmiller
Production Editor: Dawn Kilgore
Cover Design: Lee Ann Hubbard
Interior Design and Page Composition: Nicola Ruskin

This book was edited and formatted using 486 PC platforms with 8MB RAM and high-resolution, dual-page monitors. The copy was produced using WordPerfect software. The text is set in New Caledonia, and the text heads in Optima. Final camera-ready output on a 1200-dpi laser imagesetter by Pfeiffer & Company.